I0394378

Cartography Design Annual

#2

Edited by Nick Springer

Published by Springer Cartographics LLC

PO Box 72, Crosswicks, NJ, 08515

www.springercartographics.com

ISBN-13: 978-0-615-30473-1

Second Edition, First Release, December 2009

Designed by Nick Springer. Cover by Lou Cross.

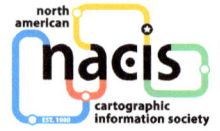

Support provided by NACIS, the North American Cartographic Information Society

www.nacis.org

Printed in USA by Lulu.com

Contents

Foreword

The 2009 Cartography Design Annual, back by popular demand, follows the inaugural issue launched by Nick Springer last year. Nick's goal, inspired by similar publications on graphic design, was to showcase maps in a printed volume designed during the previous year by members of the CartoTalk.com discussion forum and others.

The pages that follow offer maps with a variety of unique designs. There is something here for all tastes. Some maps cover grim subjects, such as Camp Delta Complex at Guantanamo Bay (page 53) appropriately depicted in monochromatic tones, and a newspaper map reporting an attempted murder on the Appalachian Trail (page 62). Other maps depict light-hearted pursuits—fun under the midnight sun to be exact, as we see in the colorful map of volleyball tournament venues in Stavanger (page 49). Who knew that a thriving beach scene exists in Norway? I am particularly fond of the numerous bird's-eye view maps found in this year's Cartography Design Annual. With their three-dimensional buildings, glittering water, and diminishing perspective — realistic elements that readers find appealing — bird's-eye views are as much about illustration as they are about cartography. The handsomely rendered map of the Stevens Institute of Technology (page 38) is one of the best maps of this type that I have seen.

Faux antique maps are another abundant category this year. I can say from hard-learned experience that creating these highly graphical maps is difficult, and a lot of fun. Designing ornate embellishments — cartouches, compass roses, sea monsters and the like — often takes as much time as the map itself, but are essential for creating a historical feel. The Uyghur map (page 13) employs a scroll motif and muted palette to evoke the history of that Central Asian crossroads.

Other maps in this volume rely less on graphical razzle-dazzle and more on their underlying data to tell a story. For example, Visualizing Airfare (page 46) shows on an equidistant map centered on London that distances flown and the price paid for a ticket are not necessarily correlated — heavily traveled routes to distant large cities cost relatively less than flying to nearby small cities. When it comes to airfares and distance, the pejorative term "fly over country" actually does exist.

The diverse offerings found in this publication are a reflection of the major changes affecting cartography. Once dominated by large organizations producing standardized maps, the profession has undergone decentralization in recent decades and has seen a growing number of small mapmaking businesses, many consisting of a single individual. Thanks to digital production, more people than ever before are making decisions about the design of the maps. This has resulted in an explosion in variety.

The contributors to this book live in one half dozen or so countries scattered around the globe. That such a geographically disparate group has collaborated points to another change in the cartography profession: our world is shrinking. Thirty years ago when I was a student distinctly different schools of cartographic design characterized geographic regions. European reference maps were easily identifiable by their great density of information compared to relatively sparse North American maps. Single line roads were the de facto standard in North America compared to double lines in Europe. Today, these regional design differences are blurring because of online communication. A cartographer from, say, Sweden, can just as easily exchange ideas with a Canadian thousands of kilometers distant as a fellow Swede in the next town (provided that at least one of the parties is bilingual). The dominance of a few mapping applications — Adobe and ESRI software produced most of the maps in this volume — plus a burgeoning inventory of map data in the public domain, has also worked to make the world of cartography smaller.

The primary value of the Cartography Design Annual is as a map design reference, for students and professionals alike. Learning how to design maps did not come easily to me — my first student map was a black and white number made with Pelikan ink, Mylar, and Zip-a-Tone. Although this map was a total disaster, making it was immensely satisfying and I vowed to improve as a map designer. One of the best ways to gain proficiency in map design, I have learned, is to emulate the work of established cartographers. The Cartography Design Annual would have shortened my learning curve had it been available when I was a student. Now as an experienced cartographer, I constantly have to resist becoming a creature of habit designing maps that are similar in style regardless of the circumstances. I see the maps in this book as a repository of ideas to spur continued growth as a map designer. I hope that you will, too.

Tom Patterson
U.S. National Park Service

Dennis McClendon, Chicago CartoGraphics

Science Chicago

More information: www.chicagocarto.com

Copyright: ©2008 Chicago CartoGraphics

Software Used: Adobe FreeHand

Part of a series of page-sized maps to show outreach efforts of Chicago's Museum of Science & Industry. The base map has been carefully simplified so that details of highways and municipal boundaries are not distracting. For the symbols showing program locations, I wanted something that could represent both physical and biological sciences, and the discovery that the hexagons could link together into a sort of molecular web intrigued me and delighted the client.

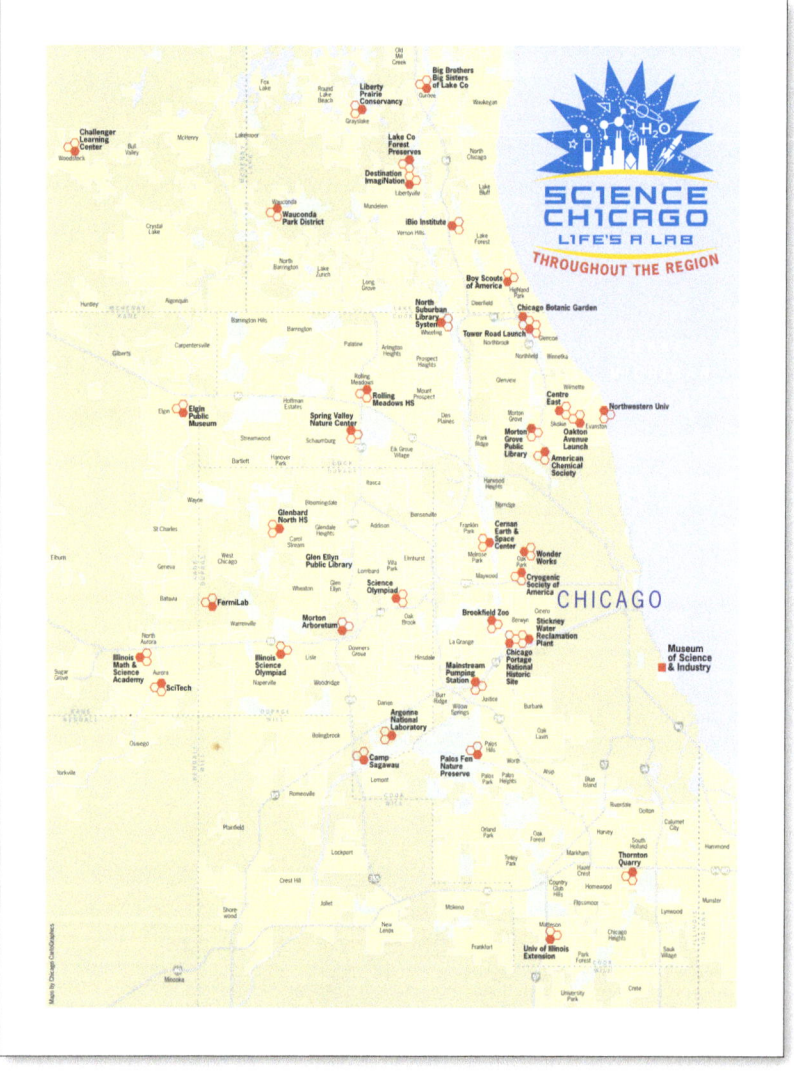

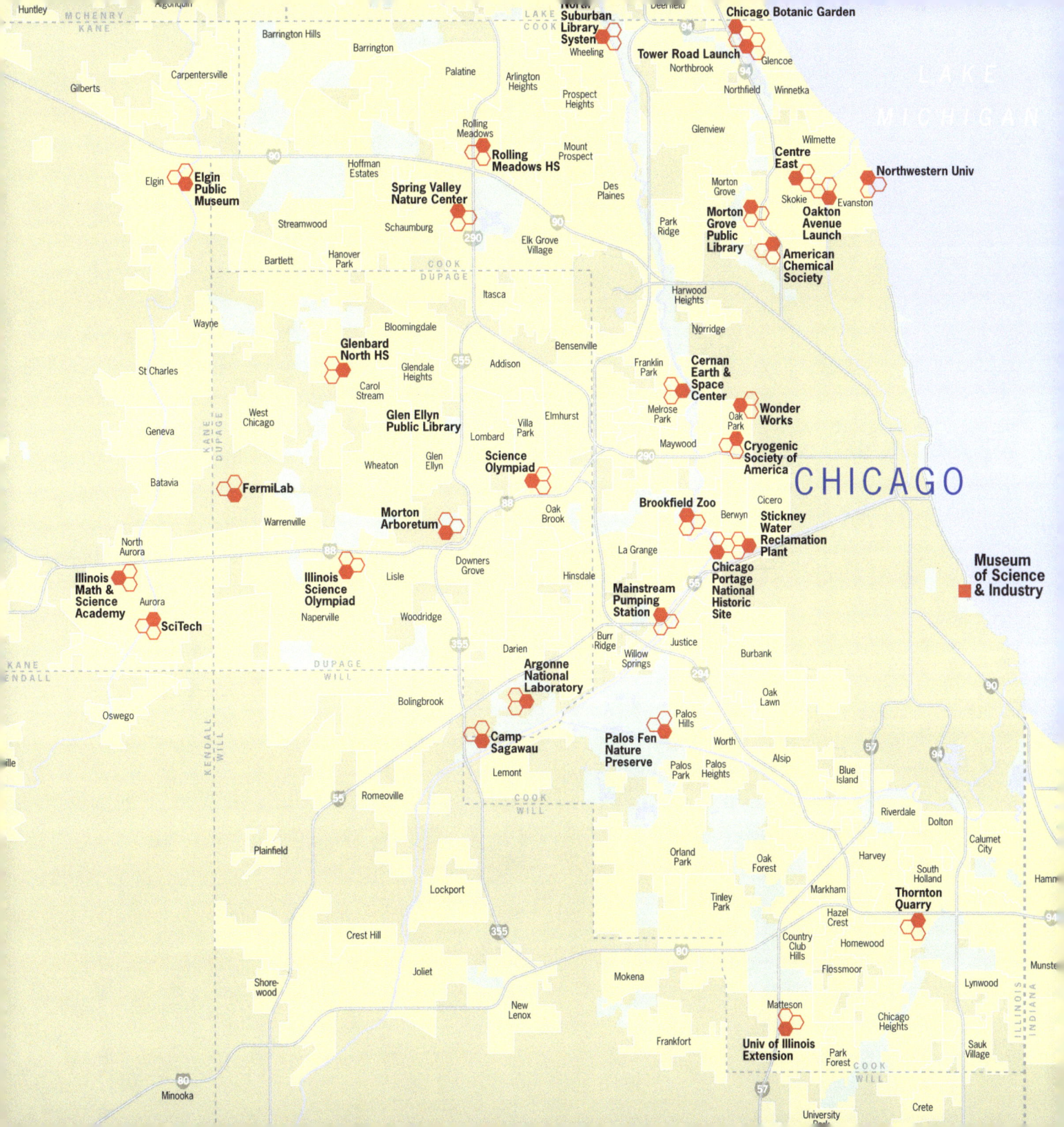

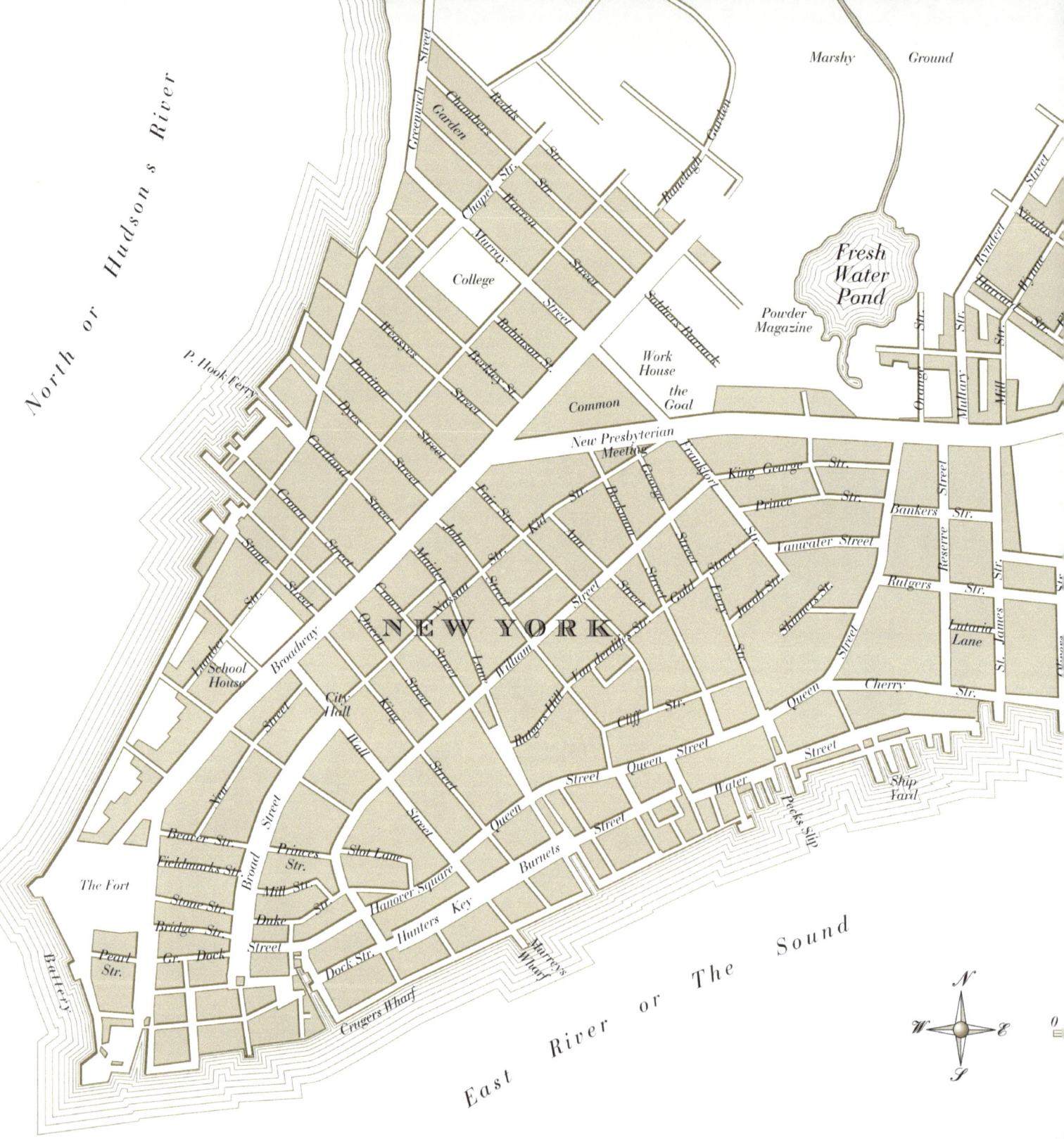

Charles Syrett, Susan Hutton, Map Graphics

New York City, 1776

More information: www.mapgraphics.com

Copyright: Copyright 2008, Heritage Muse, Inc.

Software Used: Adobe Freehand, Adobe Photoshop

This map was created as an illustration for a book with a historical theme. It is based on a map made in 1776 and is rendered in a faux antique style. Additional content was later added to the version that appears in the book.

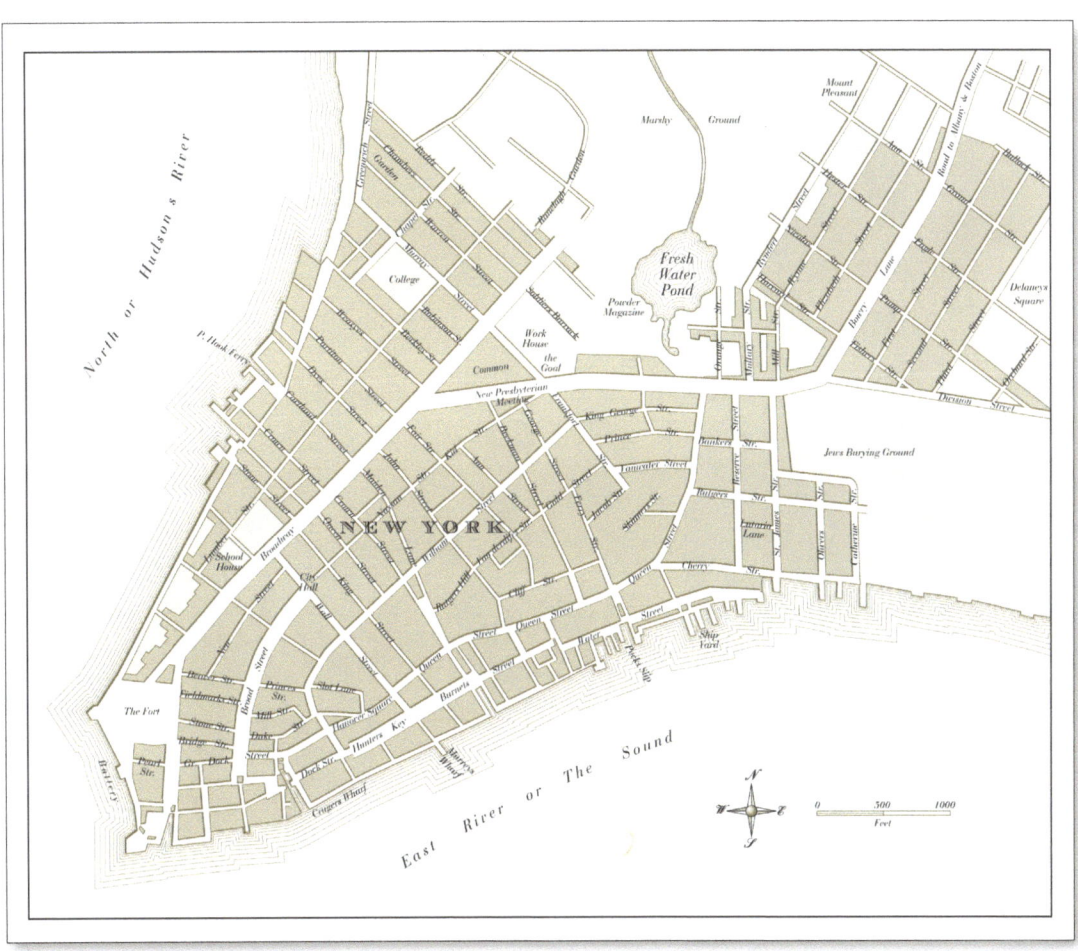

Kevin McManigal, Orange Peel Cartographic

Glacial Lake Missoula

More information: www.opcarto.com

Copyright: 2008 © Kevin McManigal

Software Used: ESRI ArcInfo, Adobe Photoshop & Illustrator

This map was designed for NACIS 2008 and shows that the conference was held at the bottom of an ancient lake. The goal was to juxtapose a prehistoric geological event with modern development and land use patterns, giving participants a sense of the natural history of the area.

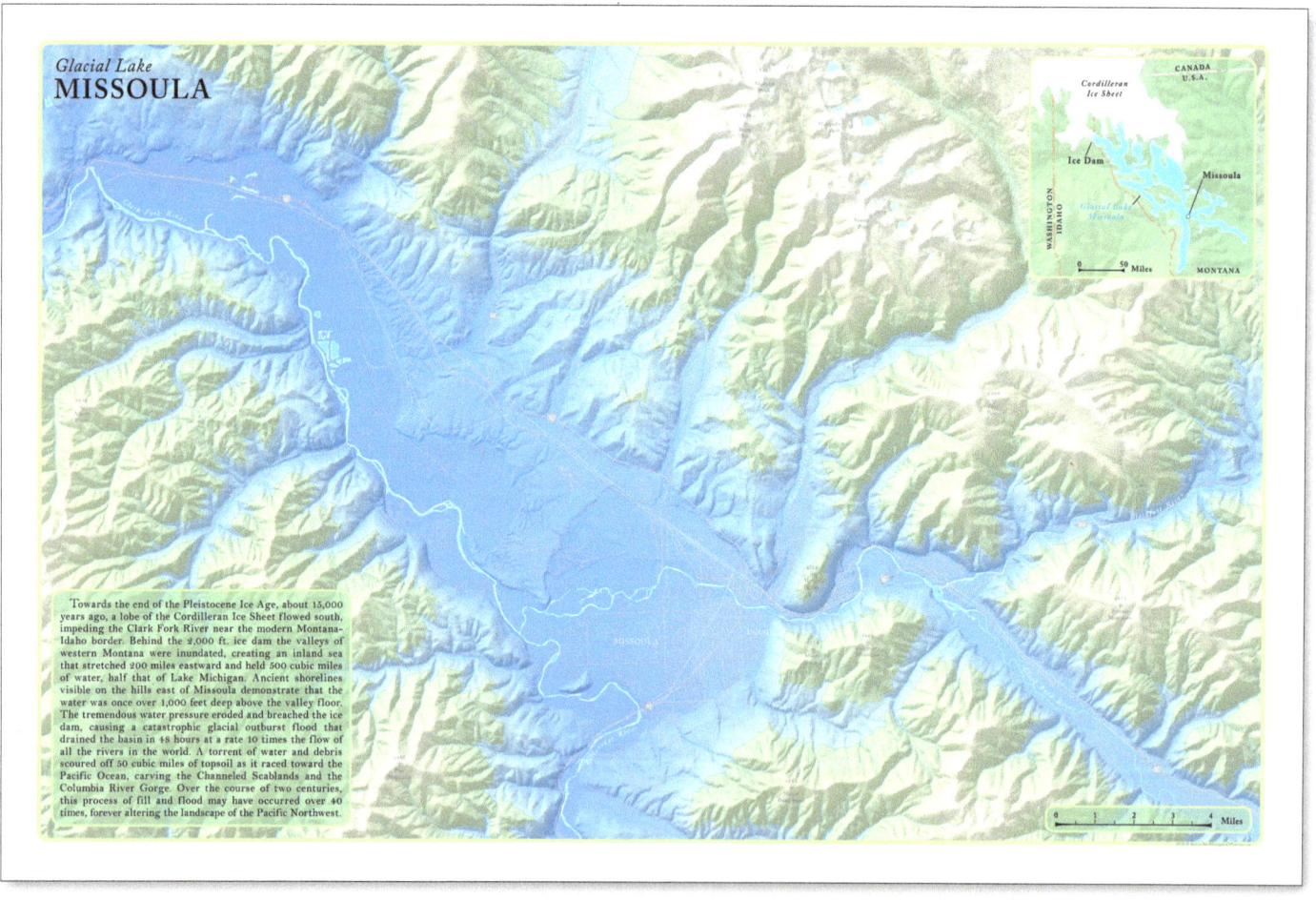

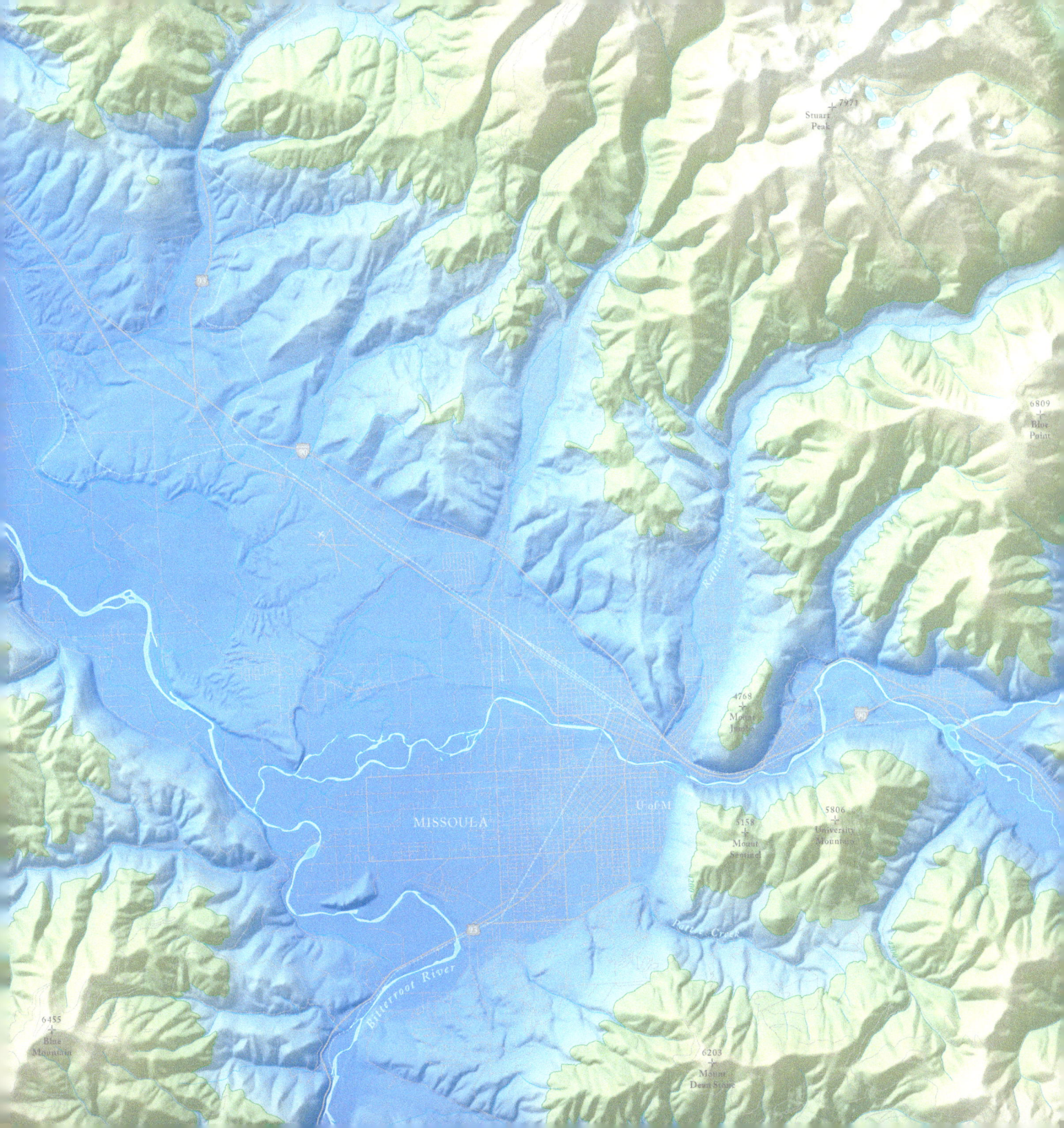

MISSOULA

U of M

Bitterroot River

+ 7973
Stuart
Peak

+ 6809
Blue
Point

Rattlesnake Creek

+ 4768
Mount
Jumbo

+ 5806
University
Mountain

+ 5158
Mount
Sentinel

Pattee Creek

+ 6455
Blue
Mountain

+ 6203
Mount
Dean Stone

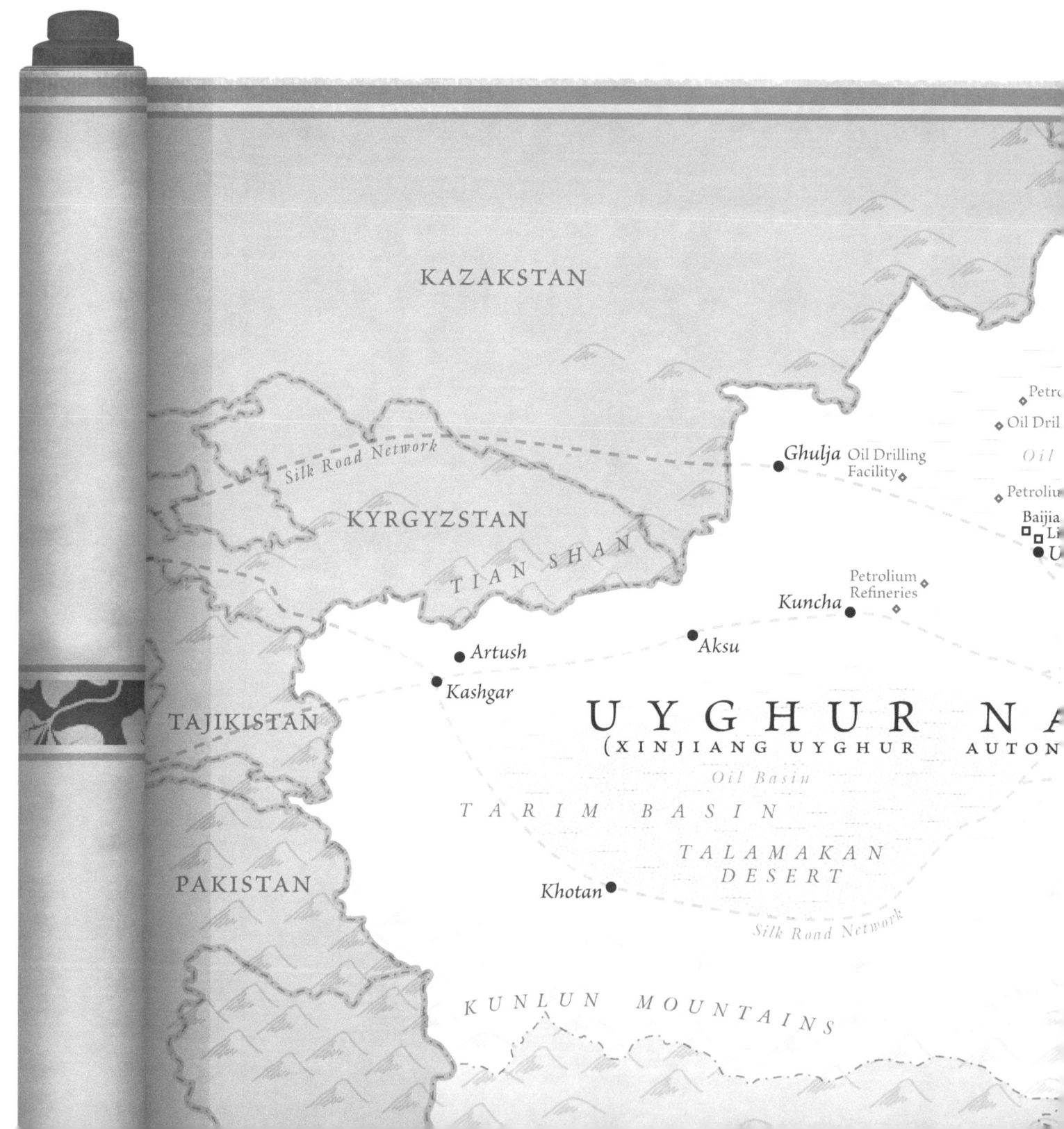

KAZAKSTAN

Petro

◇ Oil Dril

Ghulja Oil Drilling
Facility ◇

Oil

◇ Petroliu

KYRGYZSTAN

Baijia
□ Li
□
● U

Silk Road Network

TIAN SHAN

Petrolium
Refineries ◇

Kuncha ●

● *Aksu*

● *Artush*

● *Kashgar*

TAJIKISTAN

U Y G H U R   N A

(XINJIANG UYGHUR   AUTON

Oil Basin

T A R I M   B A S I N

PAKISTAN

T A L A M A K A N
D E S E R T

Khotan ●

Silk Road Network

K U N L U N   M O U N T A I N S

Casey Greene, Springer Cartographics

Uyghur

More information: www.coroflot.com/CaseyGreene

Map of Uyghur (Xinjiang Autonomous Region, China) for the book "Dragon Fighter: One Woman's Epic Struggle for Peace with China" by Rebiya Kadeer and His Holiness The Dalai Lama

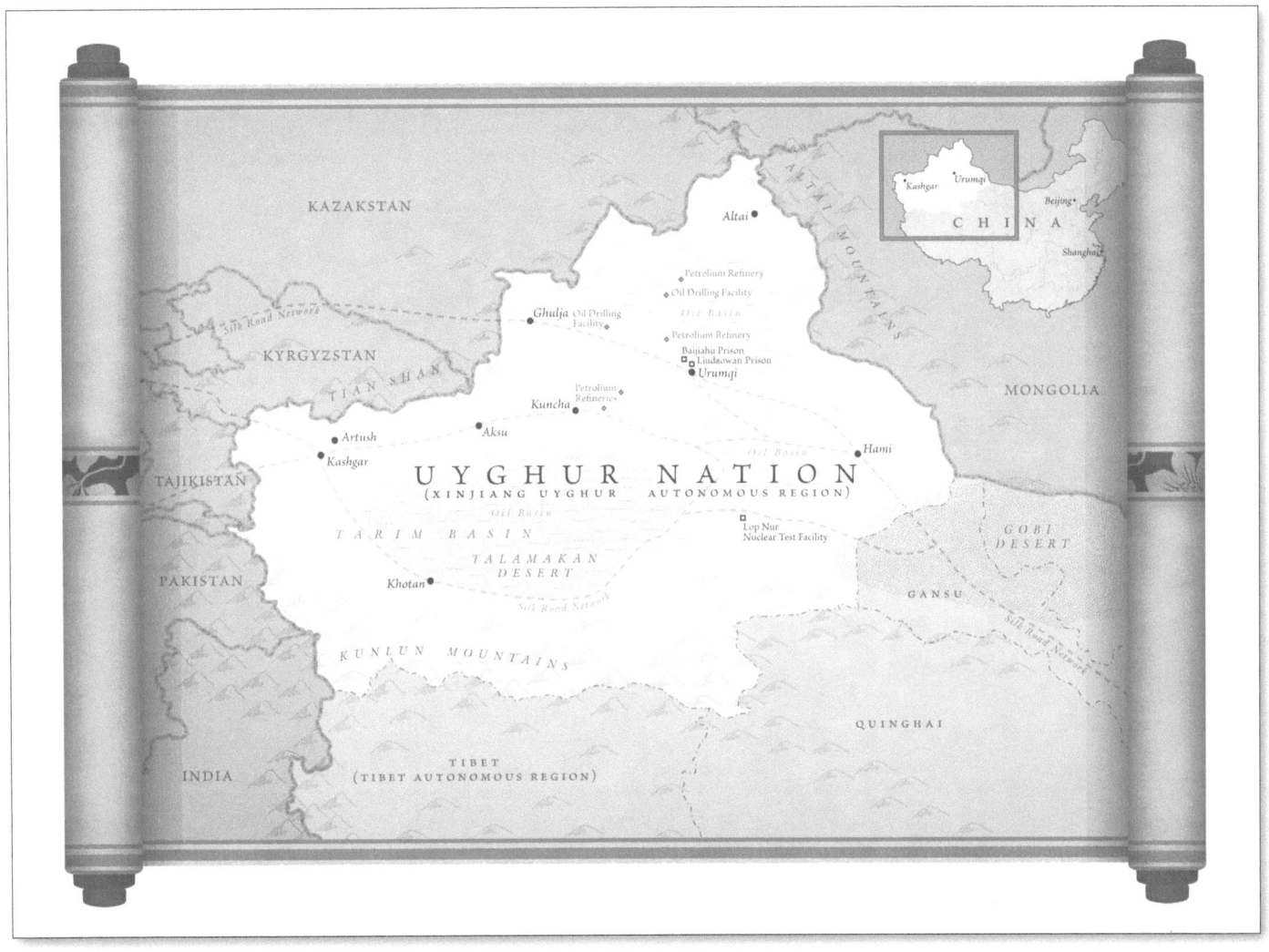

Justin Goh, Chicago CartoGraphics

O'ahu

More information: www.chicagocarto.com

Copyright: ©2008 Chicago CartoGraphics and Great Pacific Maps
Software Used: ArcMap, Adobe FreeHand

Created as a new folded map primarily for the tourist and local recreation market in O'ahu. This side shows the entire island, while the other side includes a Honolulu inset at street level, downtown with all prominent buildings and hotels shown, a University of Hawai'i campus map, and a stylized map showing local bus routes visitors can use to get around the island.

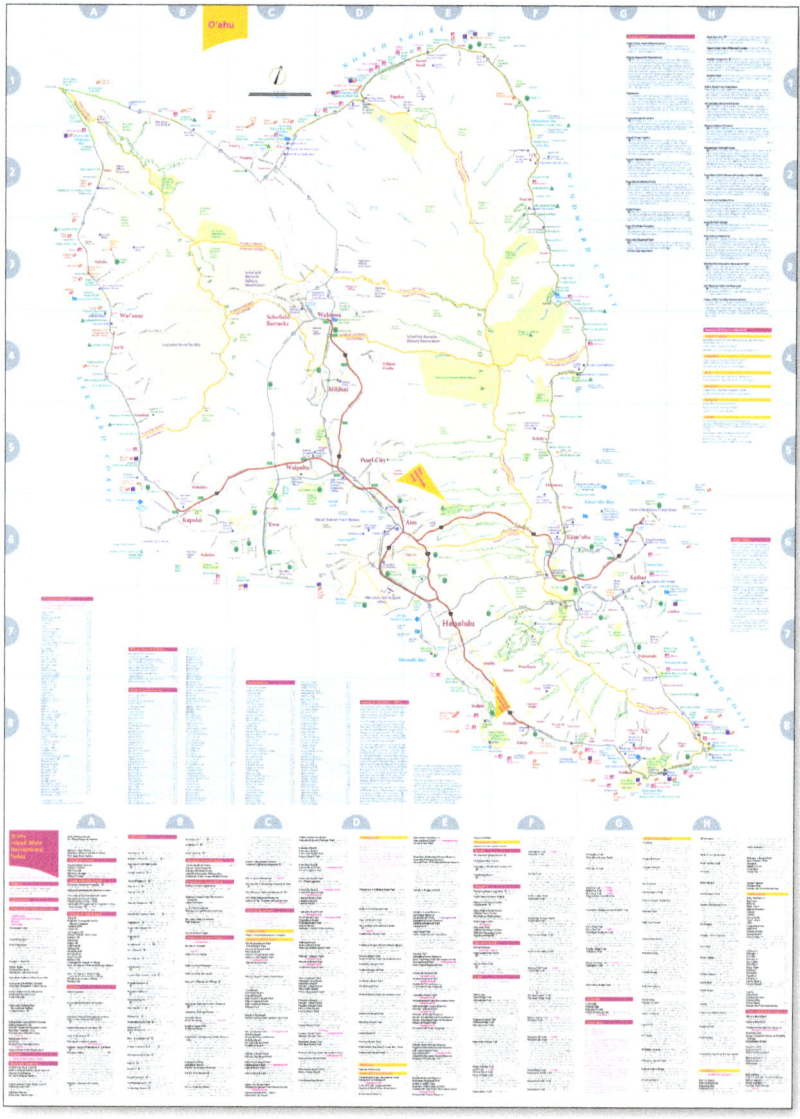

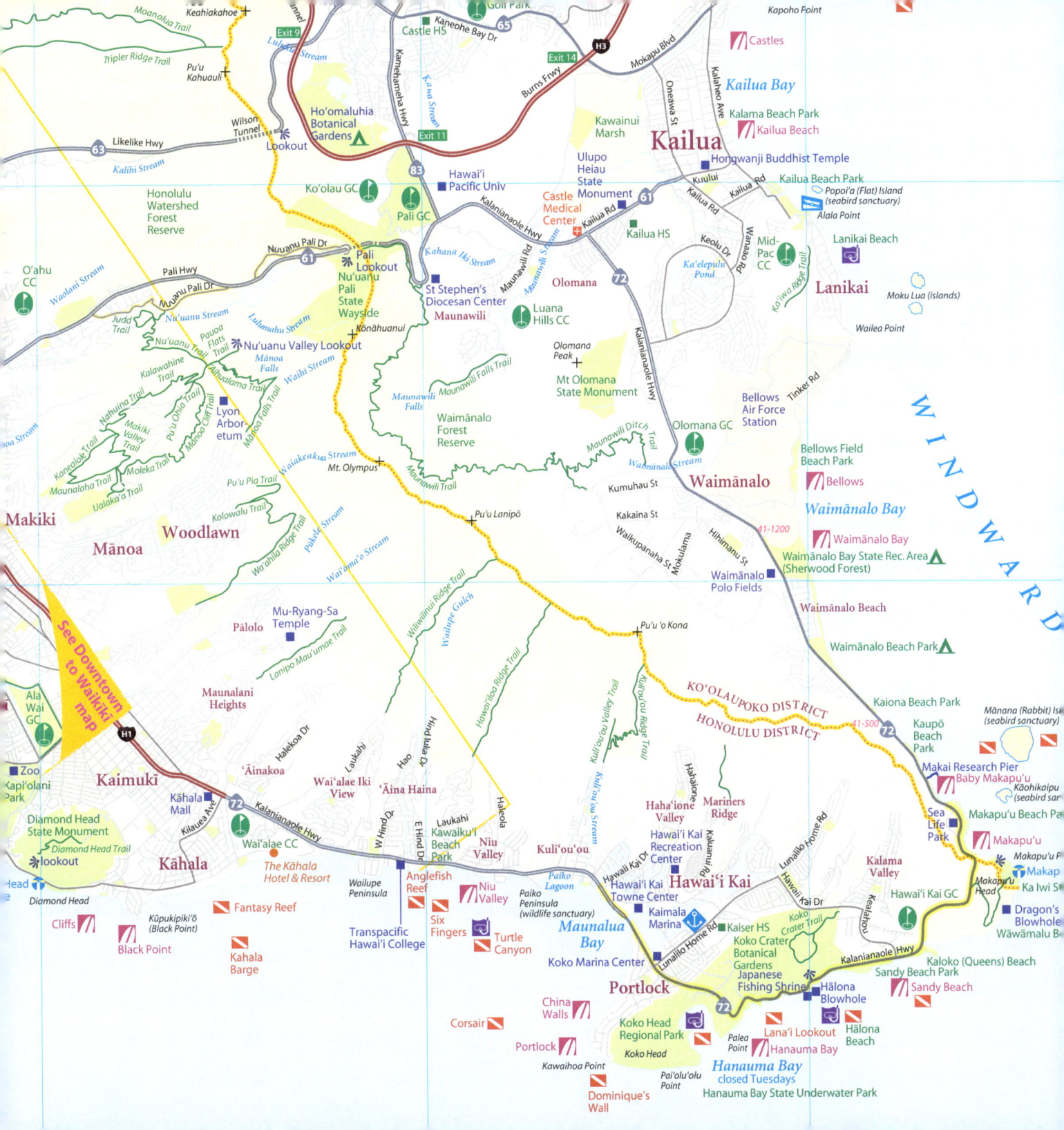

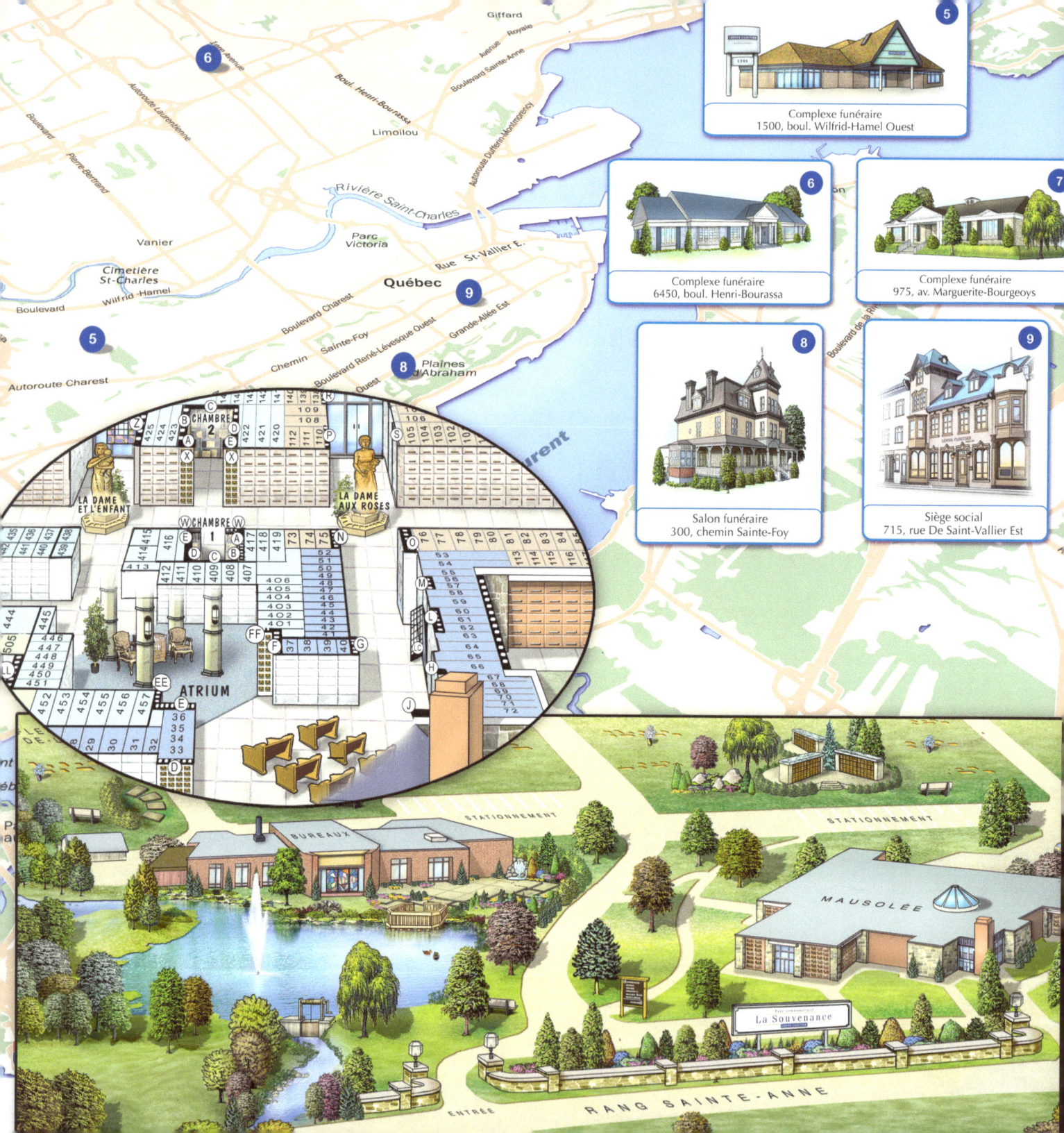

5
Complexe funéraire
1500, boul. Wilfrid-Hamel Ouest

6
Complexe funéraire
6450, boul. Henri-Bourassa

7
Complexe funéraire
975, av. Marguerite-Bourgeoys

8
Salon funéraire
300, chemin Sainte-Foy

9
Siège social
715, rue De Saint-Vallier Est

Jean-Louis Rheault

Québec Lépine-Cloutier

More information: JLRmaps@gmail.com

Software Used: Illustrator, hand drawings and Photoshop

Map showing 9 Lepine-Cloutier funeral homes in Quebec City with focus on cemetery and Mausoleum

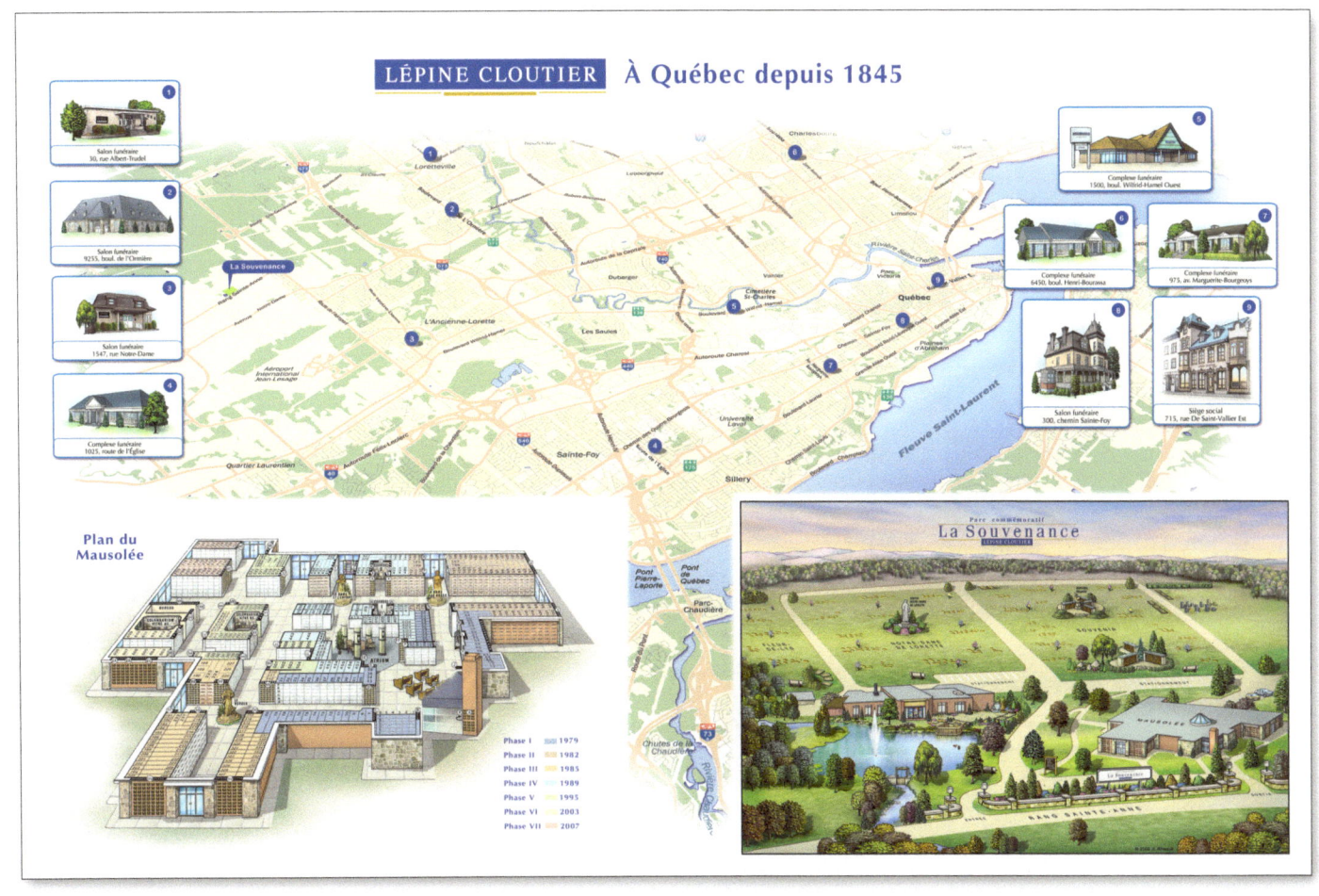

Hugo Ahlenius, UNEP/GRID-Arendal

Projected temperature increases in the Arctic due to climate change, 2090 (NCAR–CCM3, SRES A2 experiment)

Copyright: © UNEP/GRID-Arendal 2008

Software Used: Adobe Illustrator CS3, ArcGIS 9.3

More information: maps.grida.no/go/graphic/projected-temperature-increases-in-the-arctic-due-to-climate-change-2090-ncar-ccm3-sres-a2-experimen

Climate change, due to increased concentrations of greenhouse gases in the atmosphere, has lead to increased temperatures and large scale changes in the Arctic. The Arctic is seen as an early warning indicator for Global Change, and a main factor in feedback effects. This map illustrates a possible scenario for changes by the end of this century, and was prepared for an educational poster for the International Polar Year (IPY).

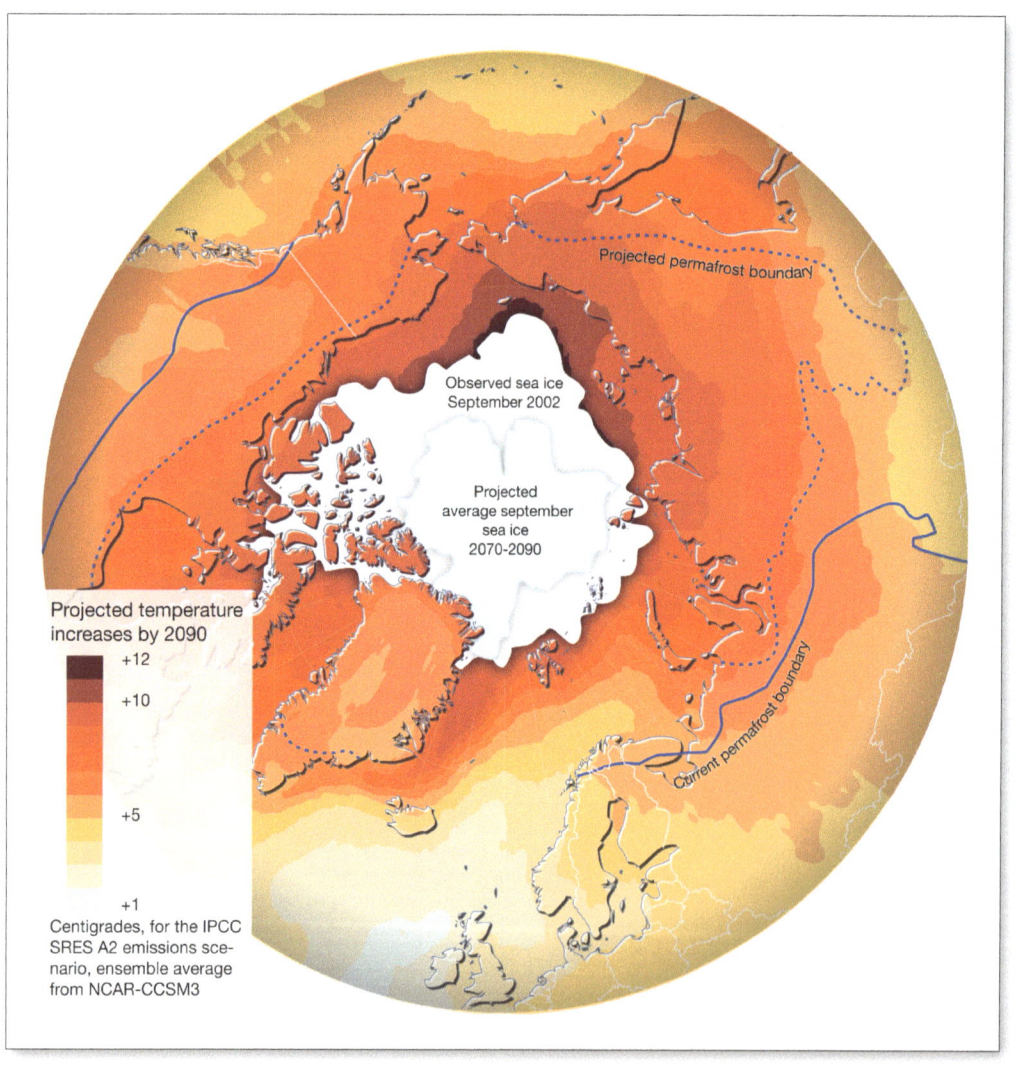

Projected permafrost boundary

Observed sea ice September 2002

Projected average september sea ice 2070-2090

Current permafrost boundary

Projected temperature increases by 2090

+12
+10

+5

+1

Centigrades, for the IPCC SRES A2 emissions scenario, ensemble average from NCAR-CCSM3

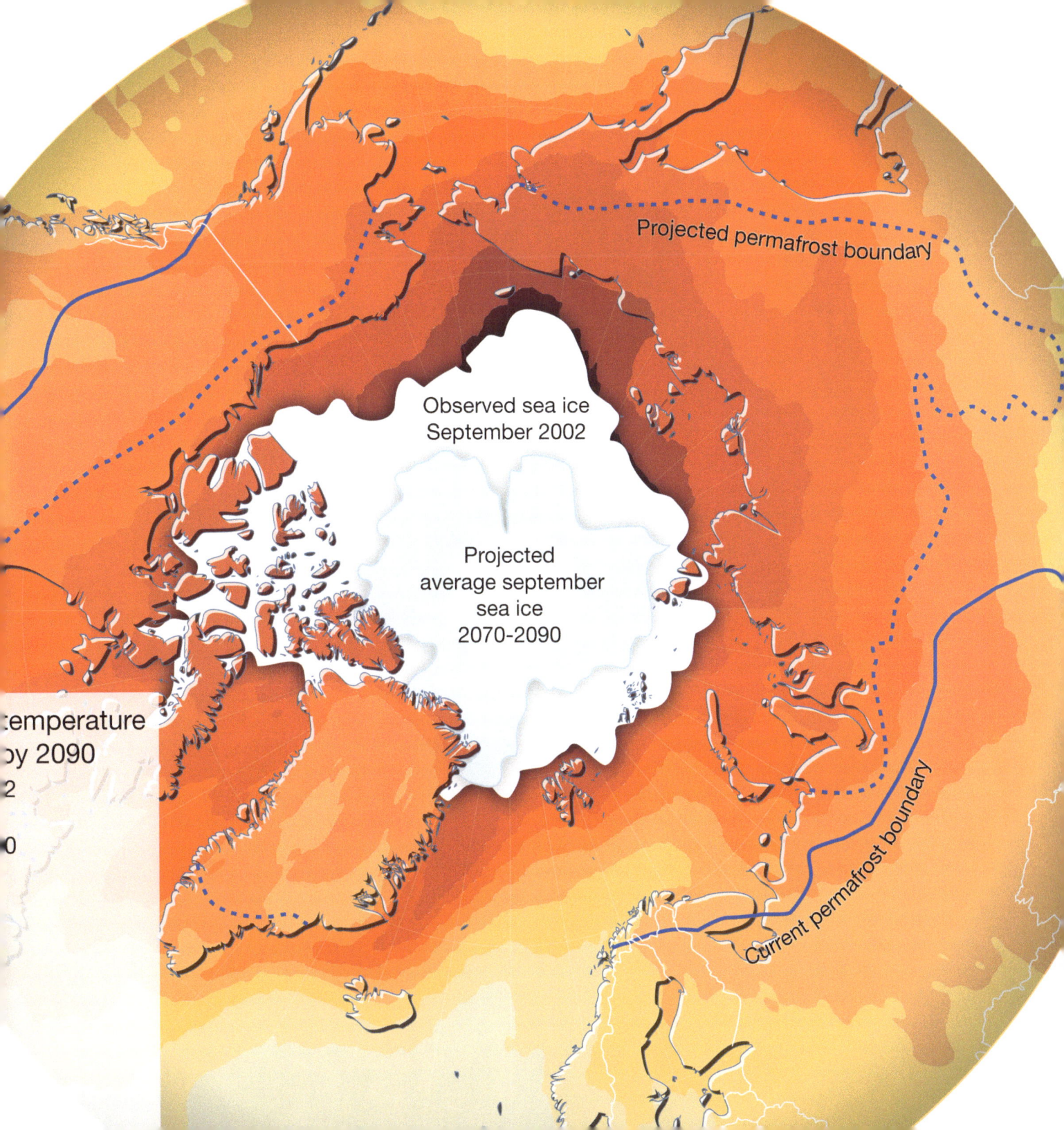

Projected permafrost boundary

Observed sea ice
September 2002

Projected
average september
sea ice
2070-2090

...emperature
...by 2090
...2
...0

Current permafrost boundary

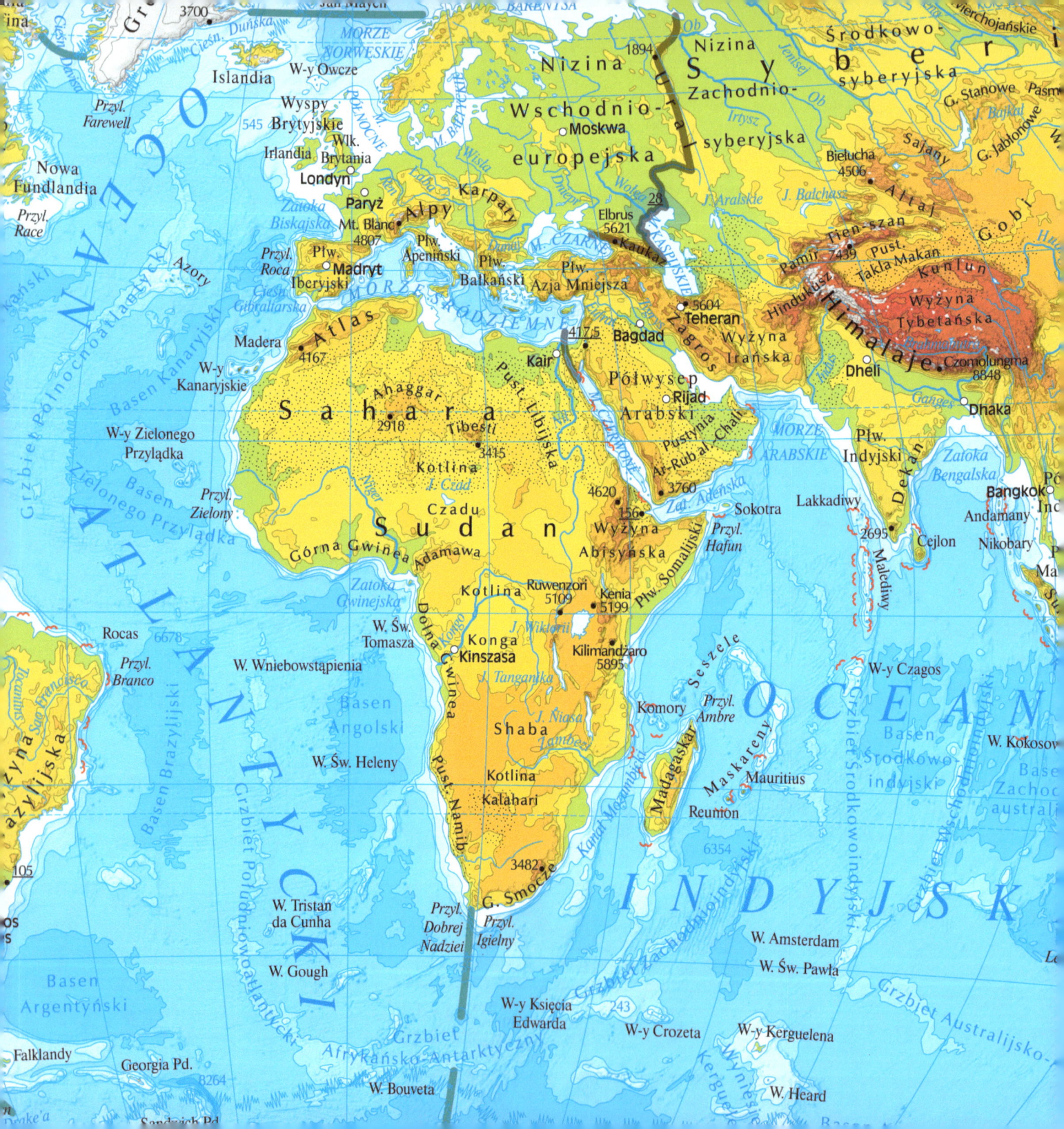

Dominik Mikiewicz, Kartografika

World Physical 100M

Copyright: 2008, Kartografika

Software Used: Manifold, MicroDEM, CorelDRAW X3

More information: www.cartomatic.pl

A physical map of the world meant to be used in atlases for higher classes of primary schools and secondary schools

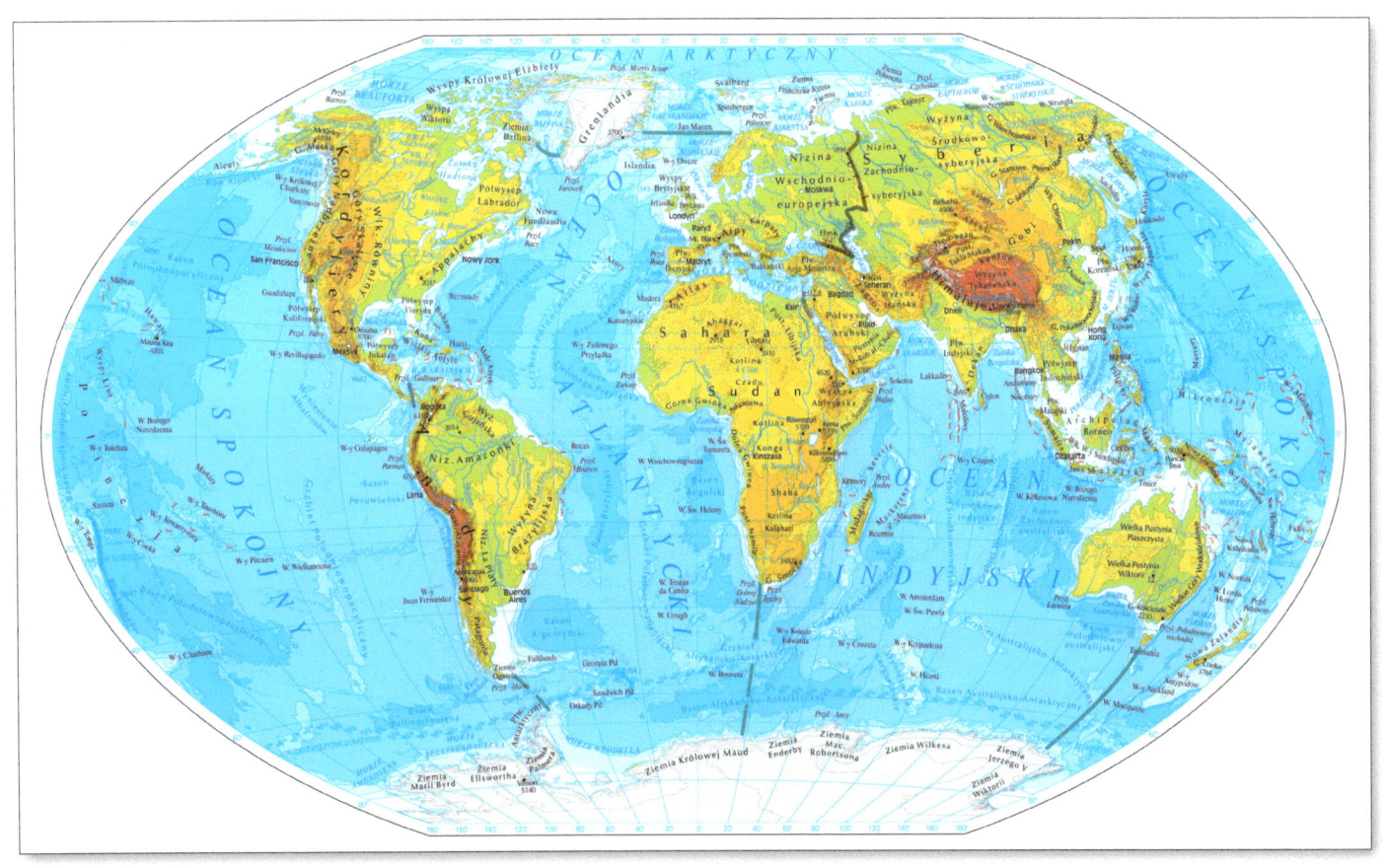

Casey Greene, Adventure Cycling Association

The Mystery of Frank Lenz

More information: www.coroflot.com/CaseyGreene

Copyright: © Casey Greene, Adventure Cyclist Magazine
Software Used: Adobe Illustrator CS3

Featured in Adventure Cyclist Magazine, this map traces the route of Frank Lenz, a young man whom in 1892 set off to ride his bicycle around the world, only to mysteriously disappear 3 years later in Kurdistan.

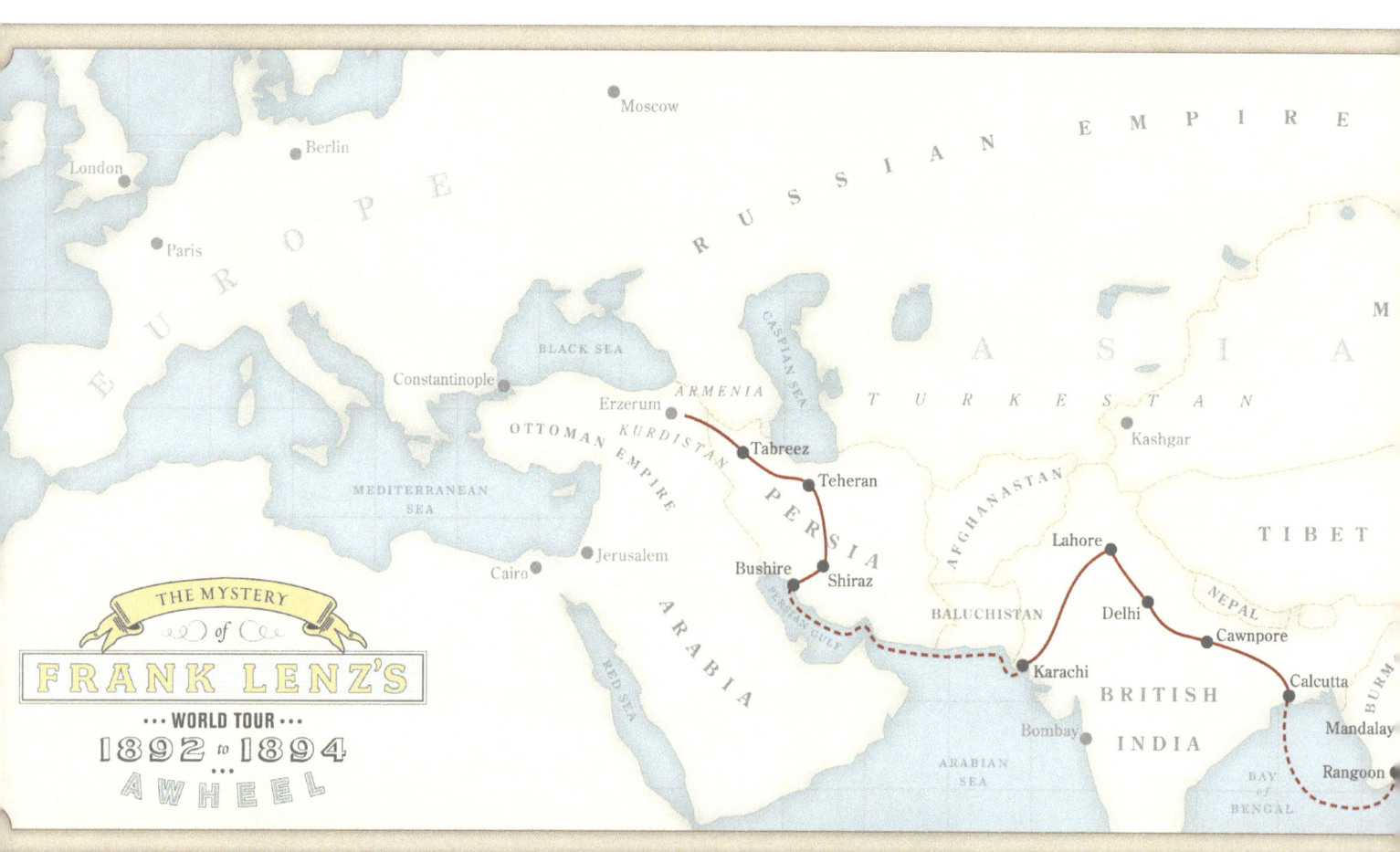

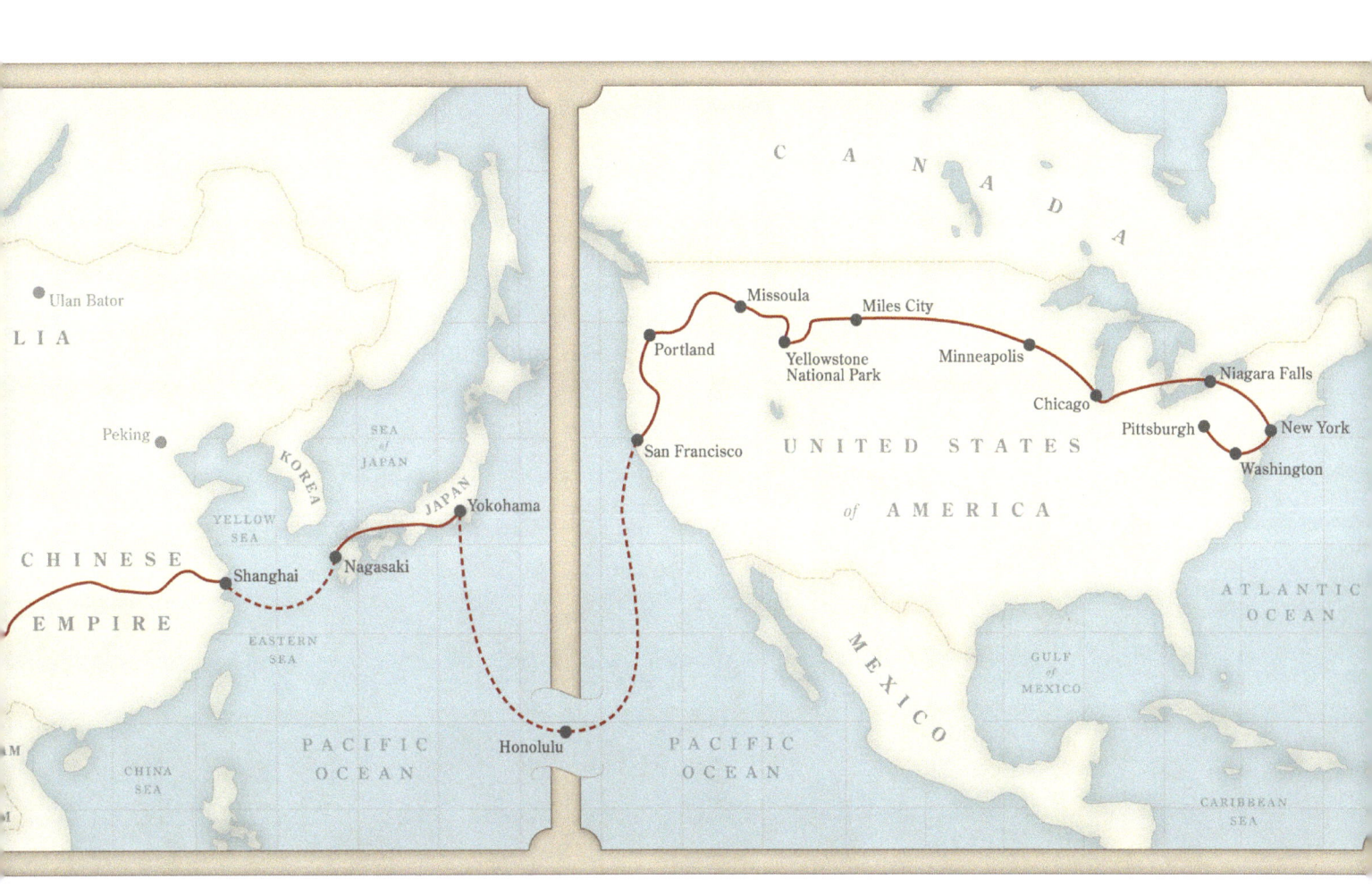

Ulan Bator

Peking

LIA

CHINESE

EMPIRE

Shanghai   Nagasaki

YELLOW
SEA

KOREA

SEA
of
JAPAN

JAPAN   Yokohama

EASTERN
SEA

CHINA
SEA

PACIFIC
OCEAN

Honolulu

San Francisco

Portland

Missoula

Yellowstone
National Park

Miles City

Minneapolis

PACIFIC
OCEAN

CANADA

UNITED STATES

of AMERICA

MEXICO

GULF
of
MEXICO

Chicago

Pittsburgh

Niagara Falls

New York

Washington

ATLANTIC
OCEAN

CARIBBEAN
SEA

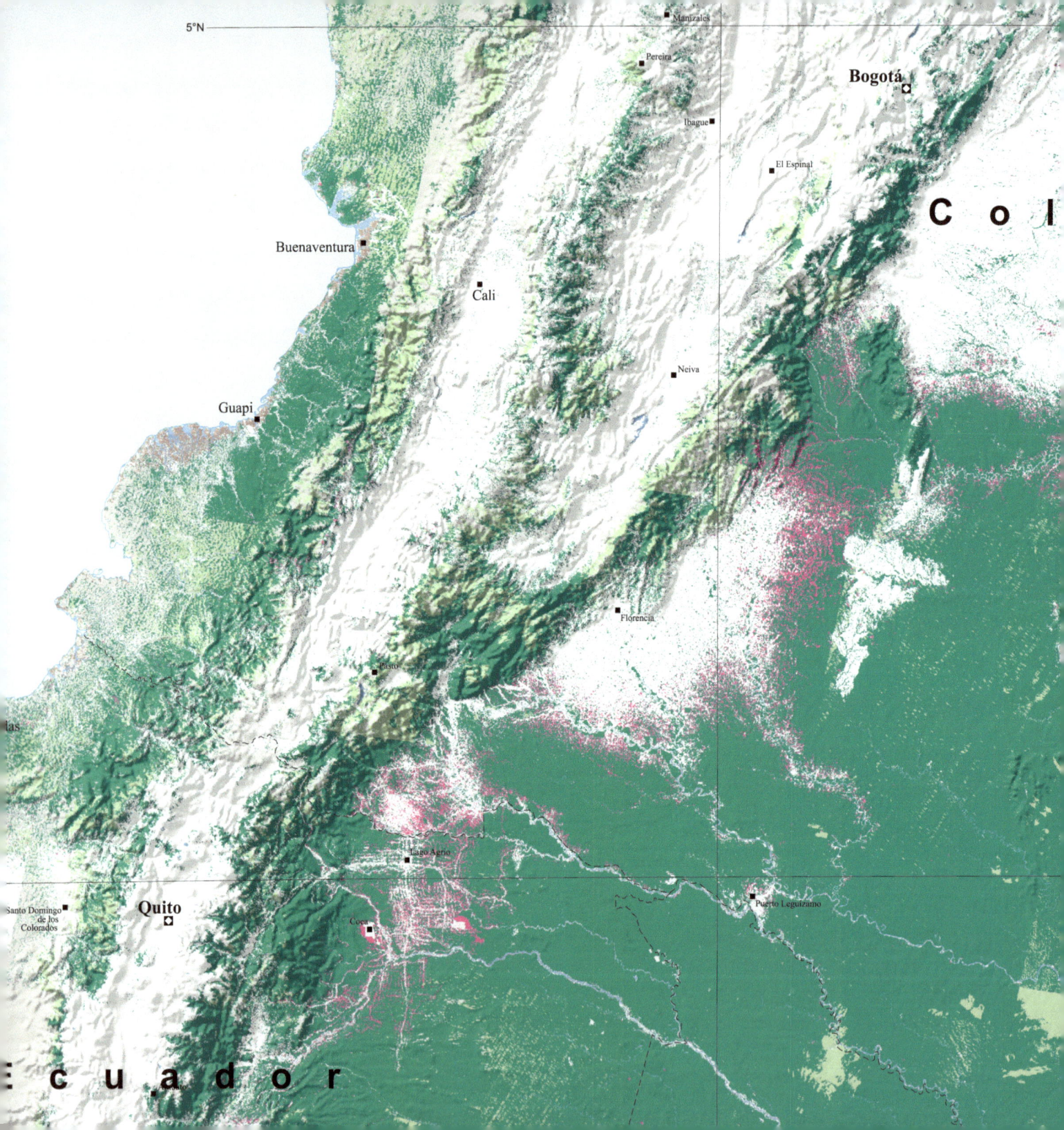

5°N

Bogotá

C o l

Manizales

Pereira

Ibague

El Espinal

Buenaventura

Cali

Neiva

Guapi

Florencia

Pasto

las

Lago Agrio

Puerto Leguízamo

Santo Domingo
de los
Colorados

Quito

Coca

E c u a d o r

Mark Denil, Conservation International

Tropical Andes: Forest Cover and Change 1990–2000

Software Used: ArcGIS, ERDAS, CorelDRAW, CorelPhotoPaint

More information: science.conservation.org/portal/
server.pt?open=512&objID=433&mode=2&in_hi_
userid=127745&cached=true

Contributors: Grady J. Harper, Marc K. Steininger, Timothy J. Killeen: Conservation International, CABS. Yamile Talero, Mayerling Sanabria: Academia Colombiana de Ciencias and Conservation International, CBC Andes. Ysaida Blanco, Oscarina Martínez, Daniel Vargas, Denisse Ramirez: SIGIS Soluciones Integrales GIS, C.A., Venezuela. Veronica Calderon, Liliana Soria, Belen Quezada: Museo de Historia Natural Noel Kempff Mercado, Bolivia.

We observed the most deforestation in Bolivia, centered on the agricultural center of Santa Cruz de la Sierra, followed closely by a large deforestation frontier in Colombia's western Amazon region and extending southward into Ecuador. Of the five countries, Ecuador lost the smallest amount of forest area, but as a portion of it's total forest area it lost the most, with 3.9% deforestation observed over the time period; Peru lost the smallest portion of it's total forest area, with a 0.7% observed loss.

Forest fragmentation is a concern in the region. By c. 2000 about 25% of the region's forests fell within a half-kilometer of a non-forest edge. Only 14% of forest was more than 8 km distant from a non-forest edge by c. 2000, a decrease of 11% since c. 1990. With the exception of Peru, very little connectivity remains between the forests of the Amazonian lowlands and the Andes. This may negatively impact the ability of species to adapt to climate change.

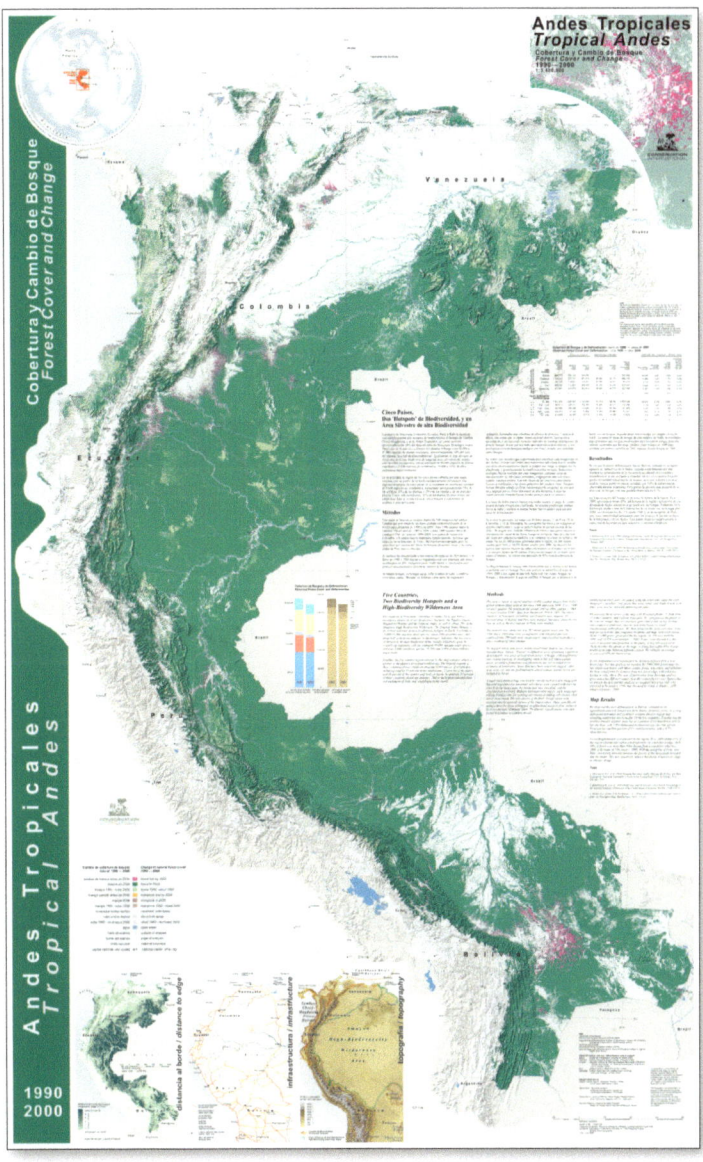

Francois Goulet, fg cartographix

Montreal, 1870

More information: www.fgcartographix.com

Copyright: Québec Amérique, 2008

Software Used: ArcGIS and MAPublisher

This is simply a locator map for an historical novel. I wanted to give it a look like the main character annotate a map she could have had. I wore for a week in my back pocket a blank piece of paper which, once scanned, was used as the background to give it a "used look." Published in: Micheline Lachance, "Les Filles tombées," Éd. Québec Amérique, 2008.

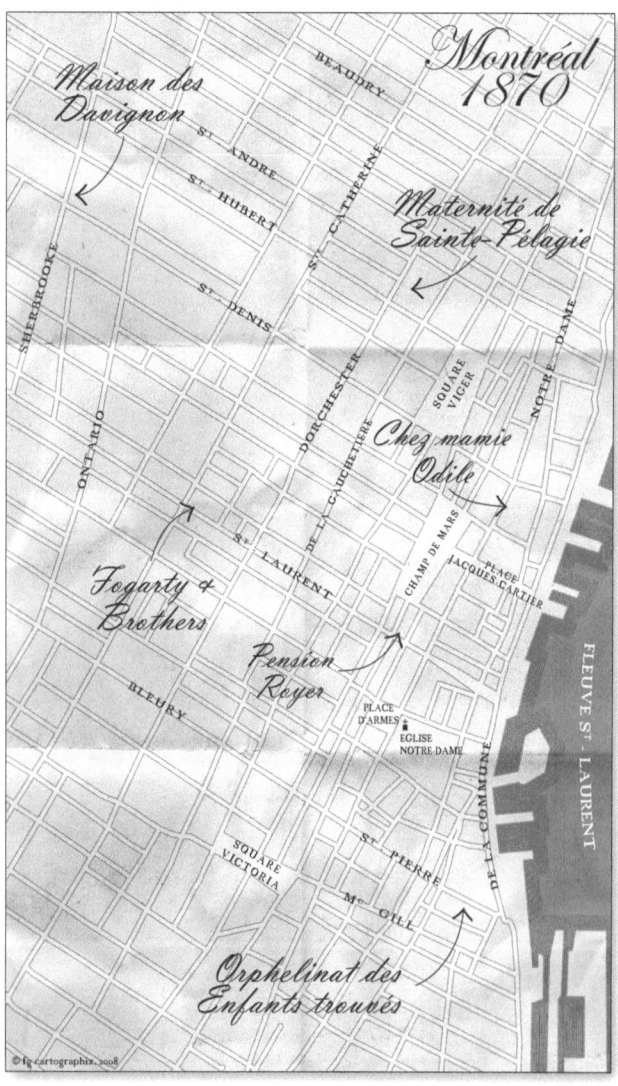

ONTARI...

DO...

DE LA GAUCHETIER

Chez mamie
Odile

St LAURENT

CHAMP DE MARS

PLACE
JACQUES-CARTIER

Fogarty &
Brothers

Pension
Royer

BLEURY

PLACE
D'ARMES

EGLISE
NOTRE-DAME

SQUARE
VICTORIA

St - PIERRE

Mc GILL

DE LA COMMUNE

FLEUVE St - LAURENT

Orphelinat des
Enfants trouvés

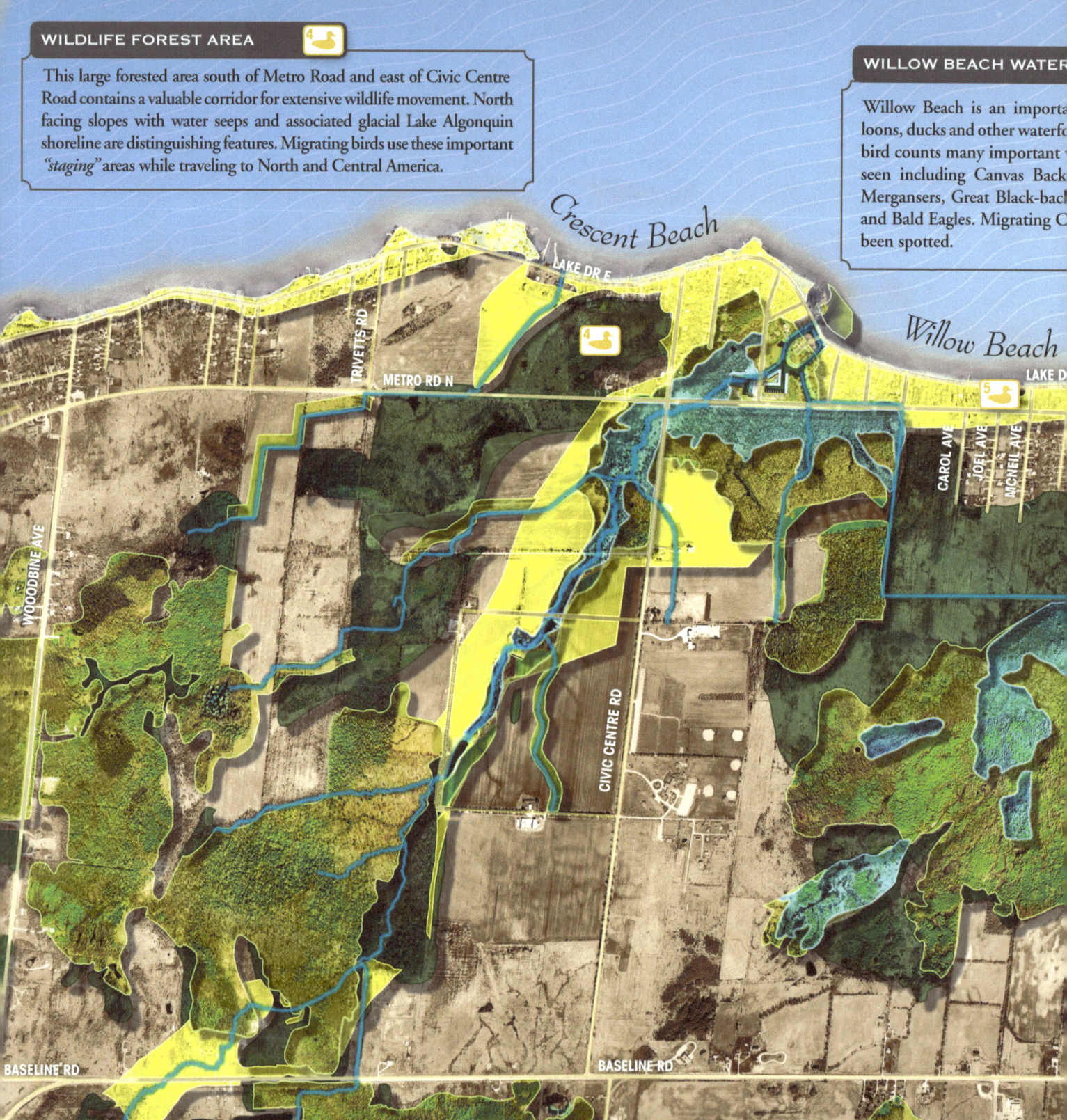

WILDLIFE FOREST AREA

This large forested area south of Metro Road and east of Civic Centre Road contains a valuable corridor for extensive wildlife movement. North facing slopes with water seeps and associated glacial Lake Algonquin shoreline are distinguishing features. Migrating birds use these important *"staging"* areas while traveling to North and Central America.

WILLOW BEACH WATER

Willow Beach is an importa
loons, ducks and other waterfo
bird counts many important
seen including Canvas Back
Mergansers, Great Black-bac
and Bald Eagles. Migrating C
been spotted.

Crescent Beach

Willow Beach

Lake Dr E

METRO RD N

Lake D

TRIVETTS RD

WOODBINE AVE

CIVIC CENTRE RD

CAROL AVE

JOEL AVE

MCNEIL AVE

BASELINE RD

BASELINE RD

Jason Anderson, Mark Setter, Daniel Faucher, Alliance for a Better Georgina

Georgina Historic Lakeshore Communities

More information: georginamaps.ca

Copyright: Map produced by the Alliance for a Better Georgina

Software Used: Avenza MAPublisher & Geographic Imager, Adobe Illustrator
& Photoshop, ArcGIS 9.1, Global Mapper 9

This map is part of a series of community maps of the Town of Georgina produced by residents. Its purpose is to showcase what residents think is important about their neighbourhood and to help protect and enhance what is special.

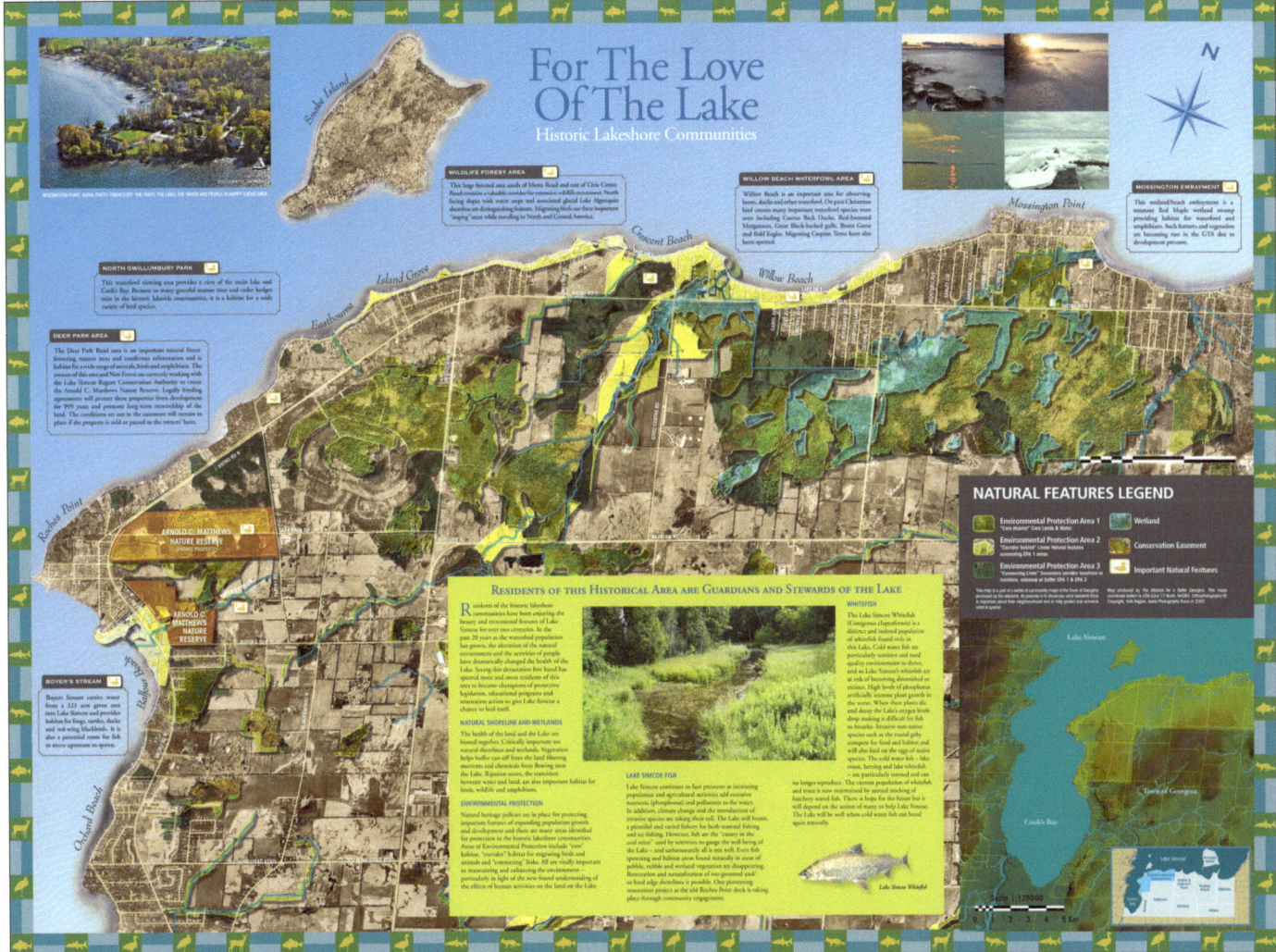

Tom Patterson, U.S. National Park Service

Denali National Park

More information: www.nps.gov

Copyright: Map is in the public domain

Software Used: MAPublisher, Natural Scene Designer, Adobe Illustrator, Adobe Photoshop

This is a remake of the Denali National Park brochure map. Colors within the park offer a simplified depiction of land cover: forest and muskeg, tundra, barren, and permanent ice and snow. Showing Mt. McKinley and the Alaska Range in a dramatic but legible fashion was a priority. To attain this goal, the map at higher elevations does not differentiate between barren and glacier land cover to give full emphasis to the shaded relief. At lower elevations the glacier tongues have greater contrast augmented with satellite image textures as they emerge from the snowy Alaska Range.

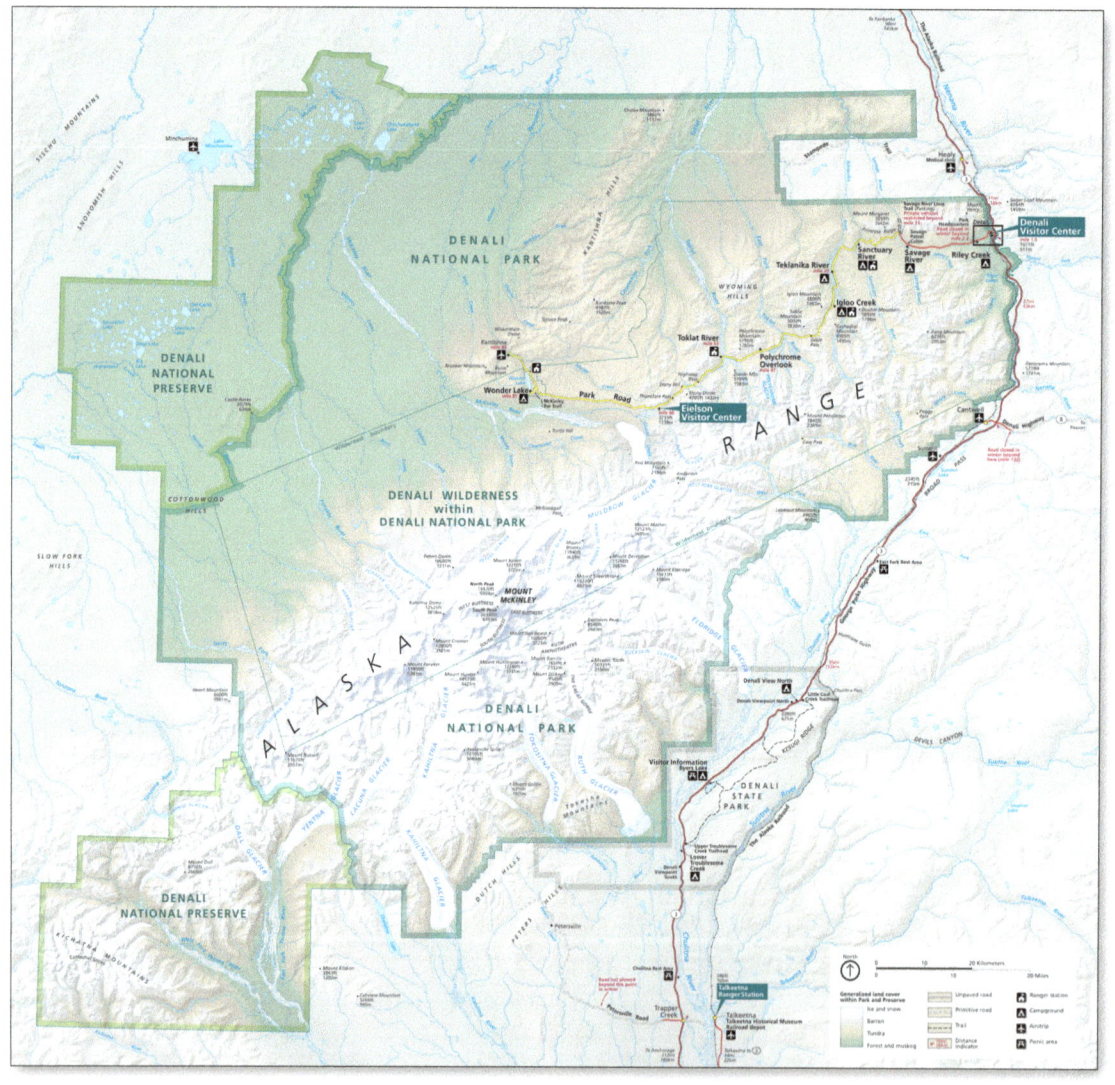

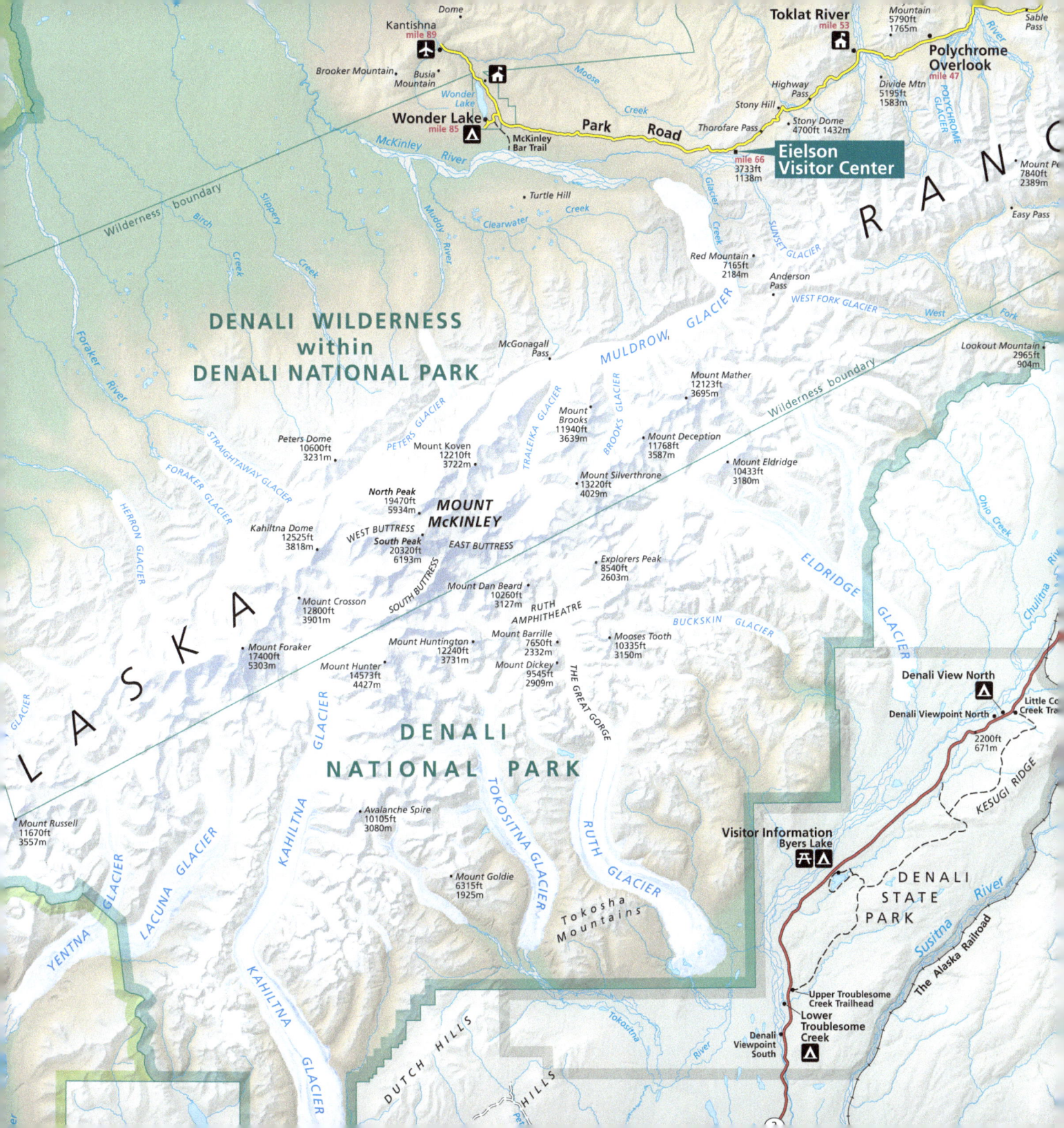

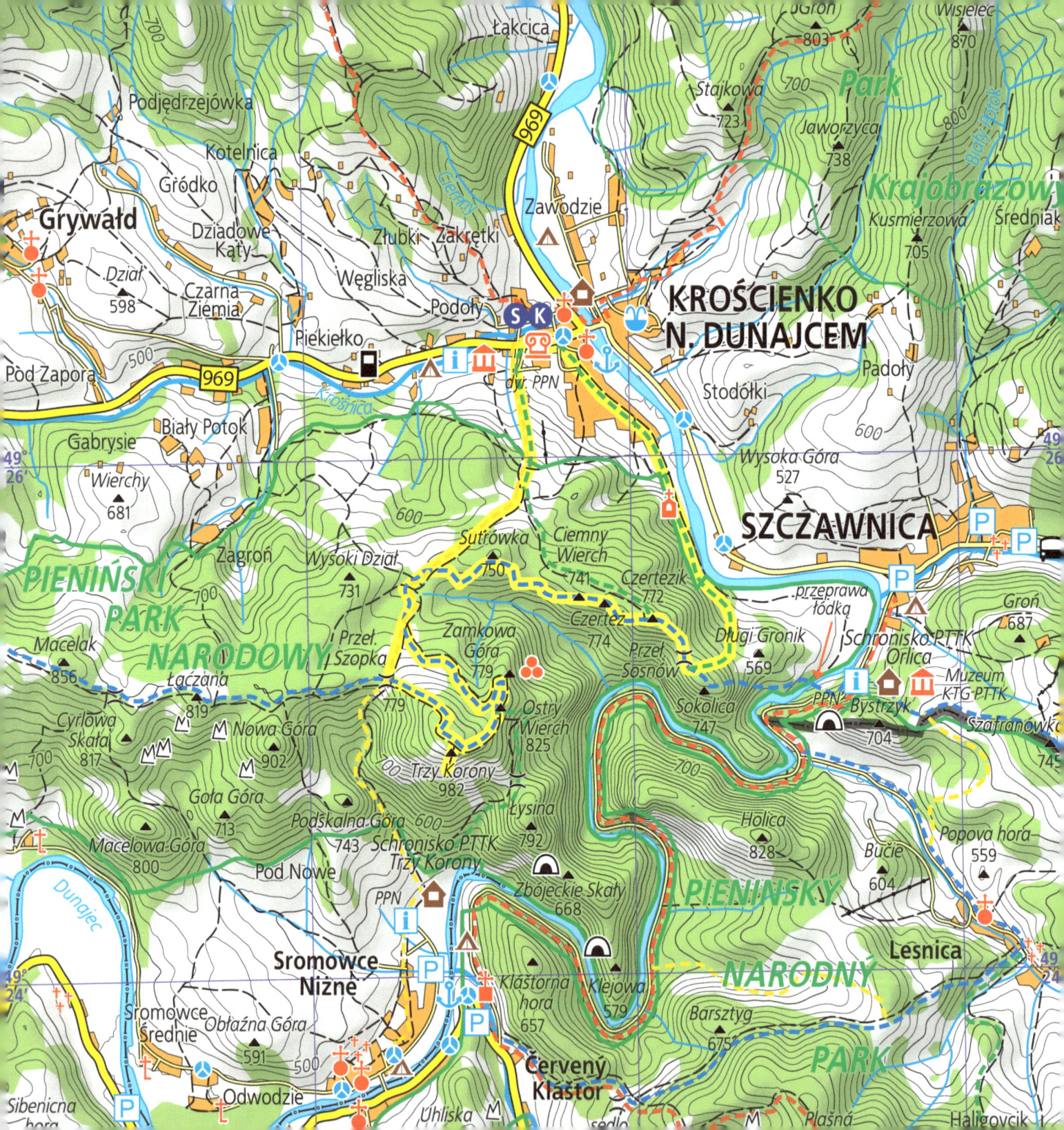

Grzegorz Marchut, Szymon Pernal, Bezdroza sp. z o.o.

Pieniny – trasa 7

More information: www.bezdroza.pl

Copyright: @Bezdroża

Software Used: Manifold 8.0., Adobe Illustrator CS3, Adobe Photoshop CS3, Microdem.

Map is a part of a mountain guide illustrating route described in text part. Data used: old topographic maps, SRTM, GPS data.

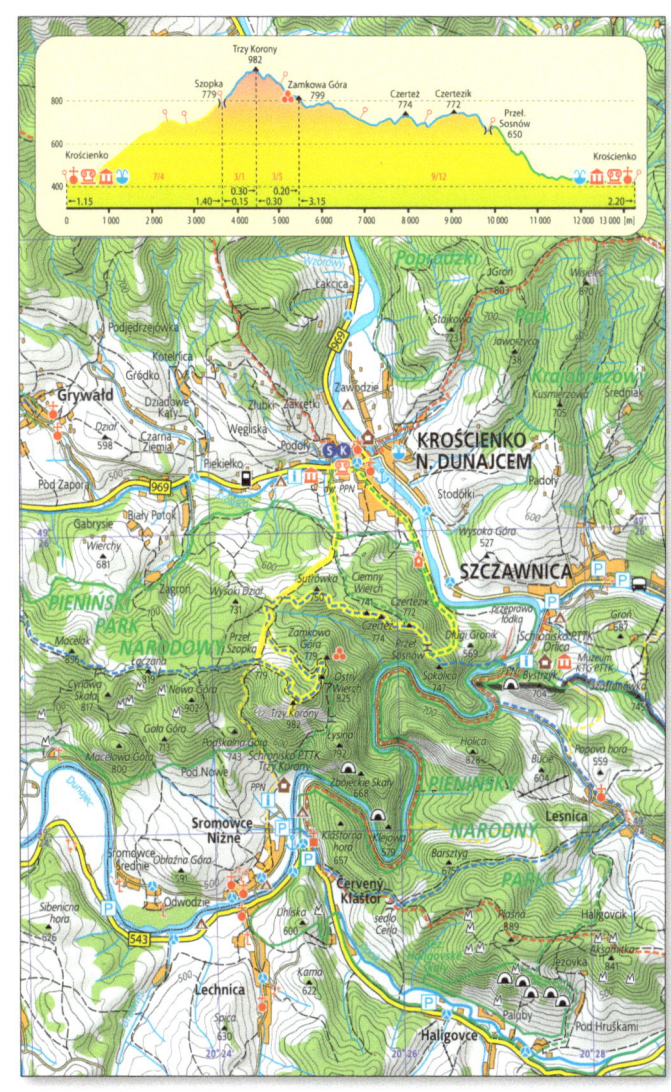

Jean-Louis Rheault and François Rheault, Illustra-Map

Dorval

More information: JLRmaps@gmail.com

Copyright: © Illustra Map Enr. 2008

Software Used: hand drawings and Photoshop

Promotional map showing a suburb community in the Montreal area.

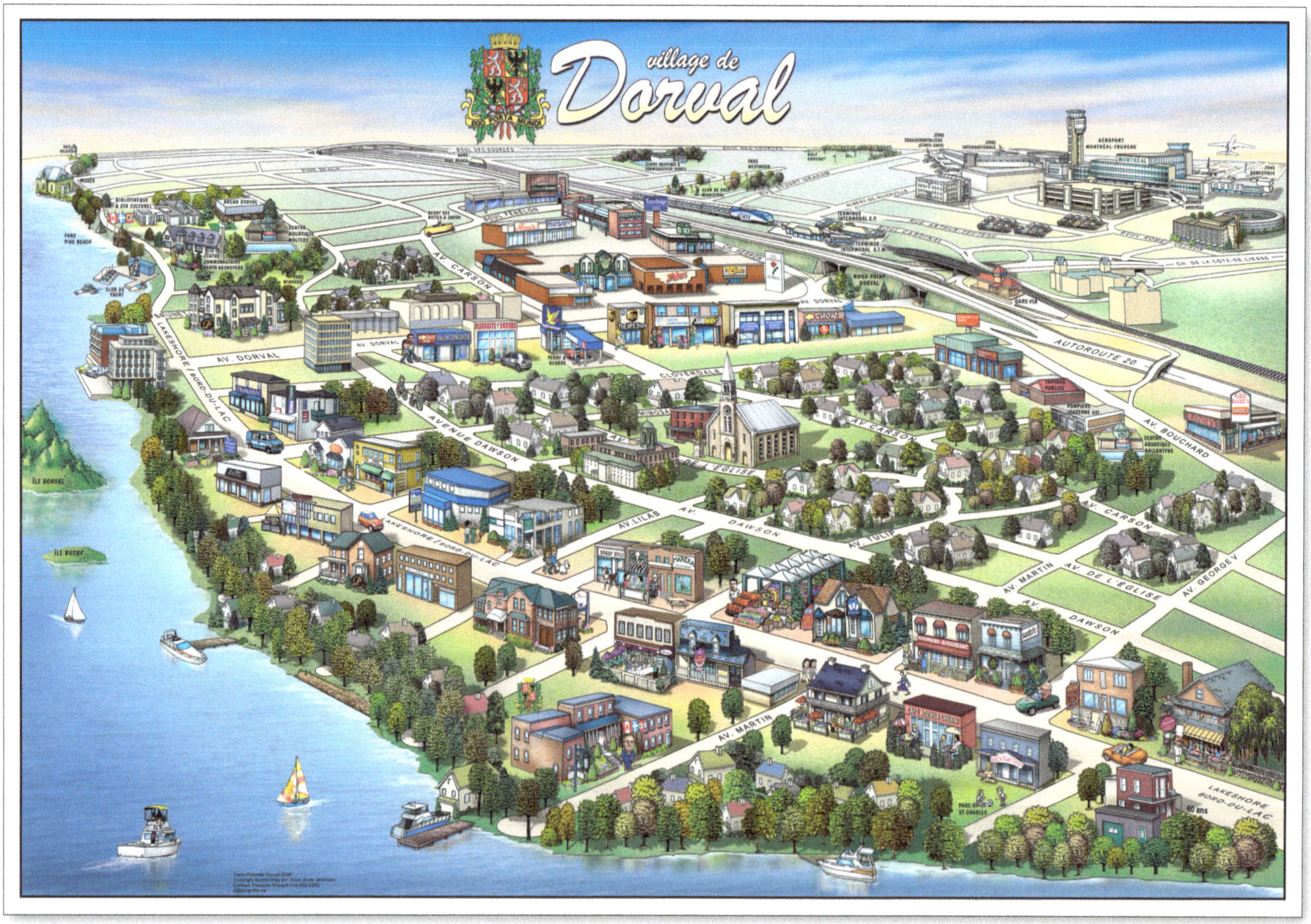

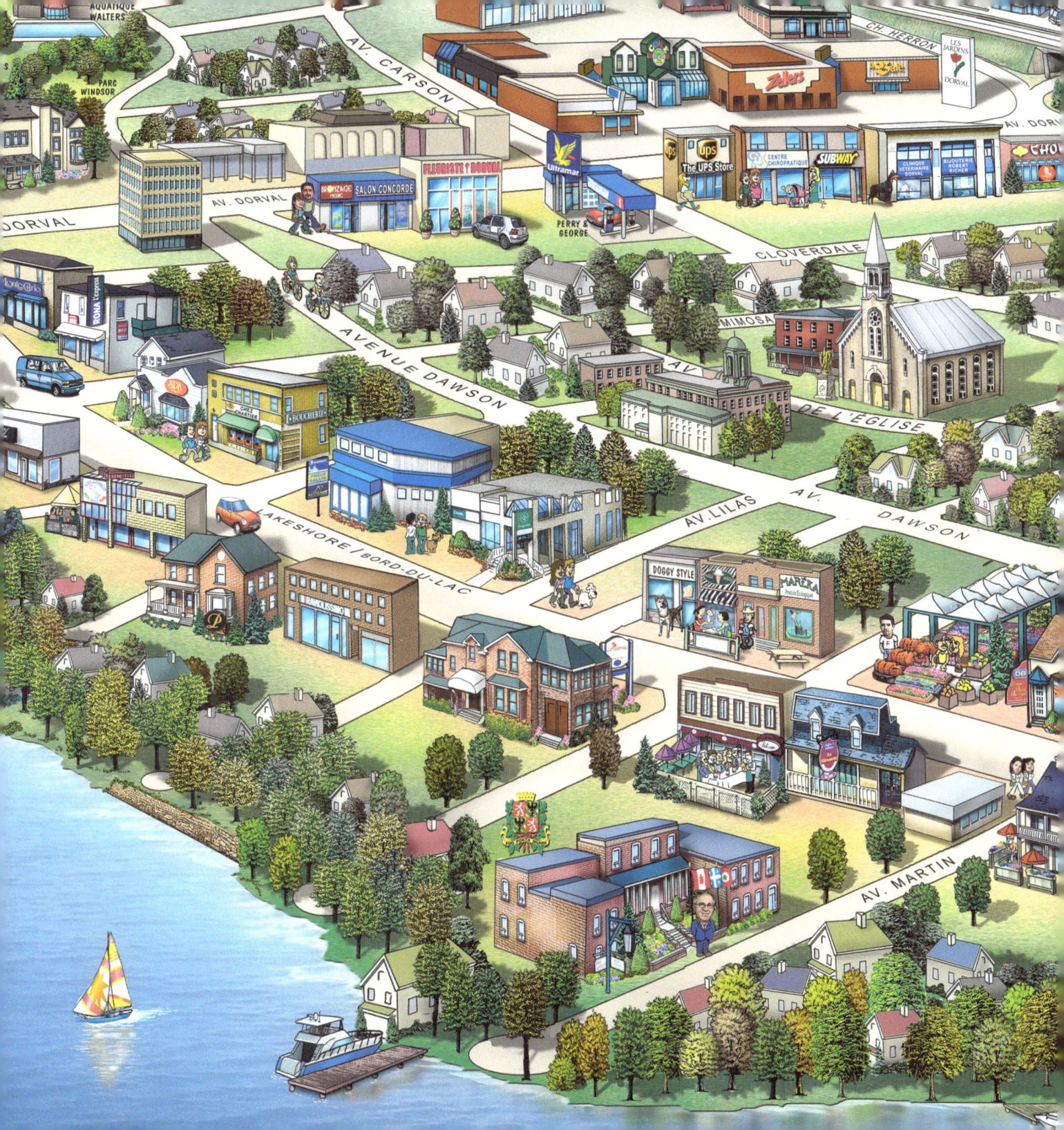

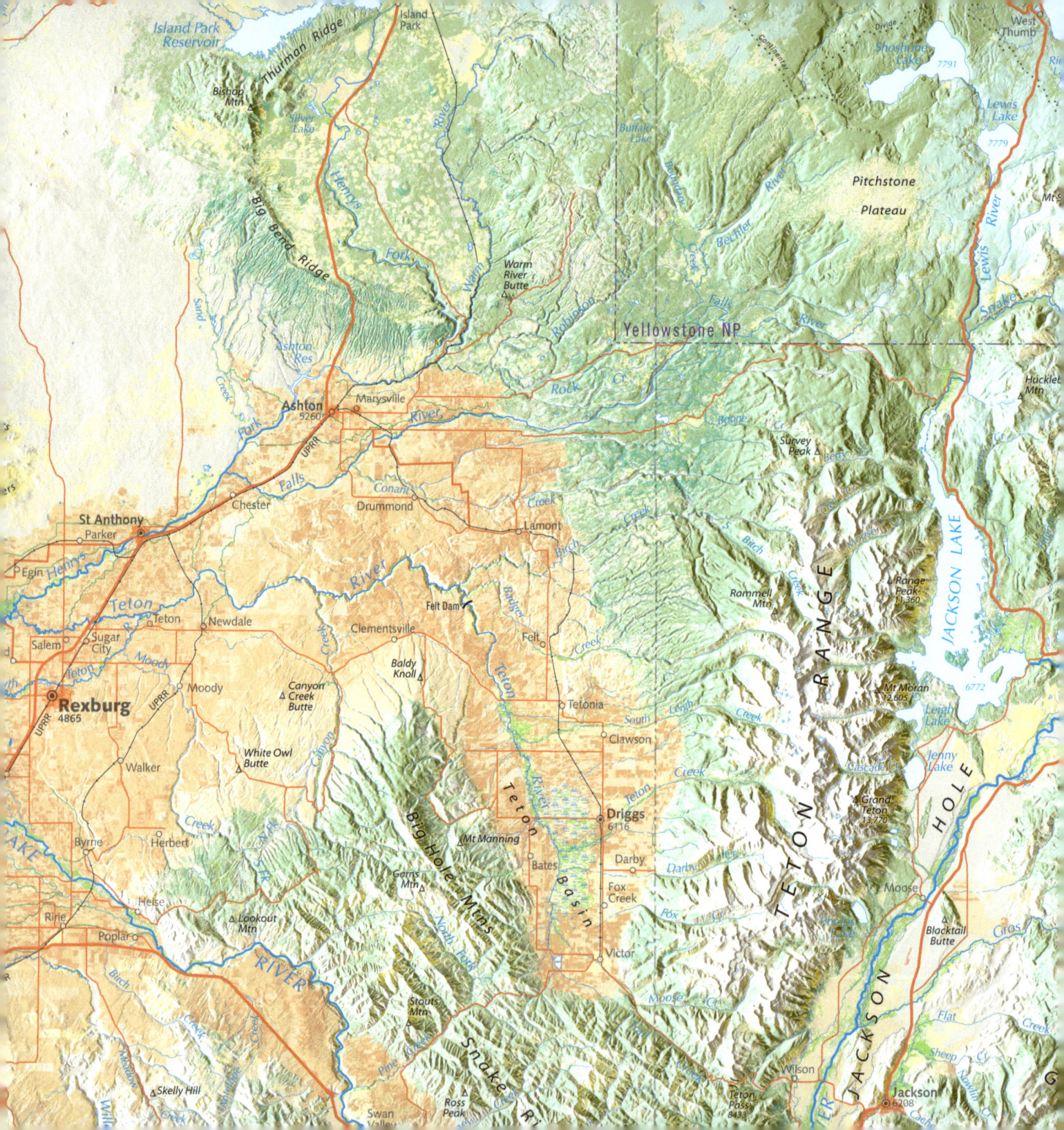

Allan Cartography Inc. and Yellowstone Ecological Research Center

The Greater Yellowstone Ecosystem

More information: www.AllanCartography.com

Copyright: Yellowstone Ecological Research Center 2008

Software Used: FreeHand, PhotoShop, ArcGIS, GlobalMapper

In 1996, we manually created the first edition of this poster which featured hypsometric tints over relief-shading. Now, this fully digital map is in it's second edition. We combined the NLCD from 1992 and 2001 to create a landscape rich with texture and color. The type was compiled to the USGS 500K state map series using the GNIS. Drainage and roads were similarly compiled from various digital vector data sources. This poster was a collaborative effort with the Yellowstone Ecological Research Center, who sells it through their website; www.yellowstoneresearch.org

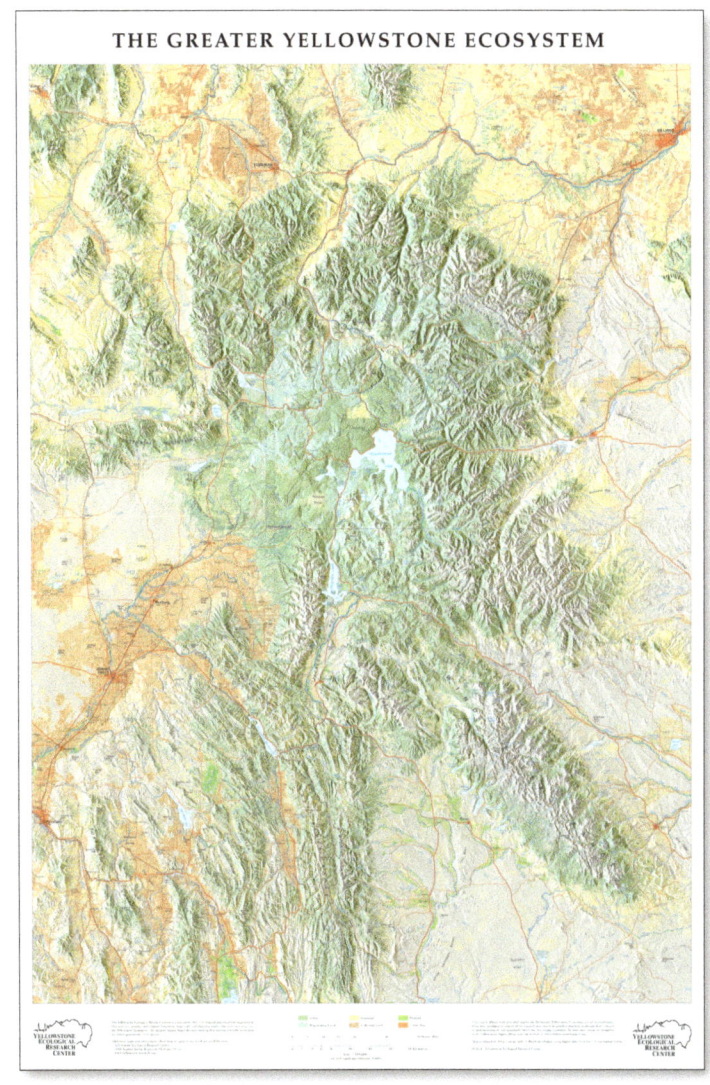

Michael Karpovage, mapformation LLC & George Bordner, Bordner Aerials

Steven Institute of Technology 3D raster style campus map

Copyright: 2008 Stevens Institute of Technology

Software Used: Adobe Photoshop CS3

More information: www.mapformation.com/portfolio/campus/
stevensIT3D.htm

New Jersey based Stevens Institute of Technology called on Mapformation to develop a 3D raster style campus map illustration for use in print, signage and web-based projects. Michael Karpovage used an oblique angle aerial photograph from Bordner Aerials as the base reference for this Photoshop illustration. Multiple layers were created, including special filter techniques and precise hand rendering using a Wacom pen and tablet.

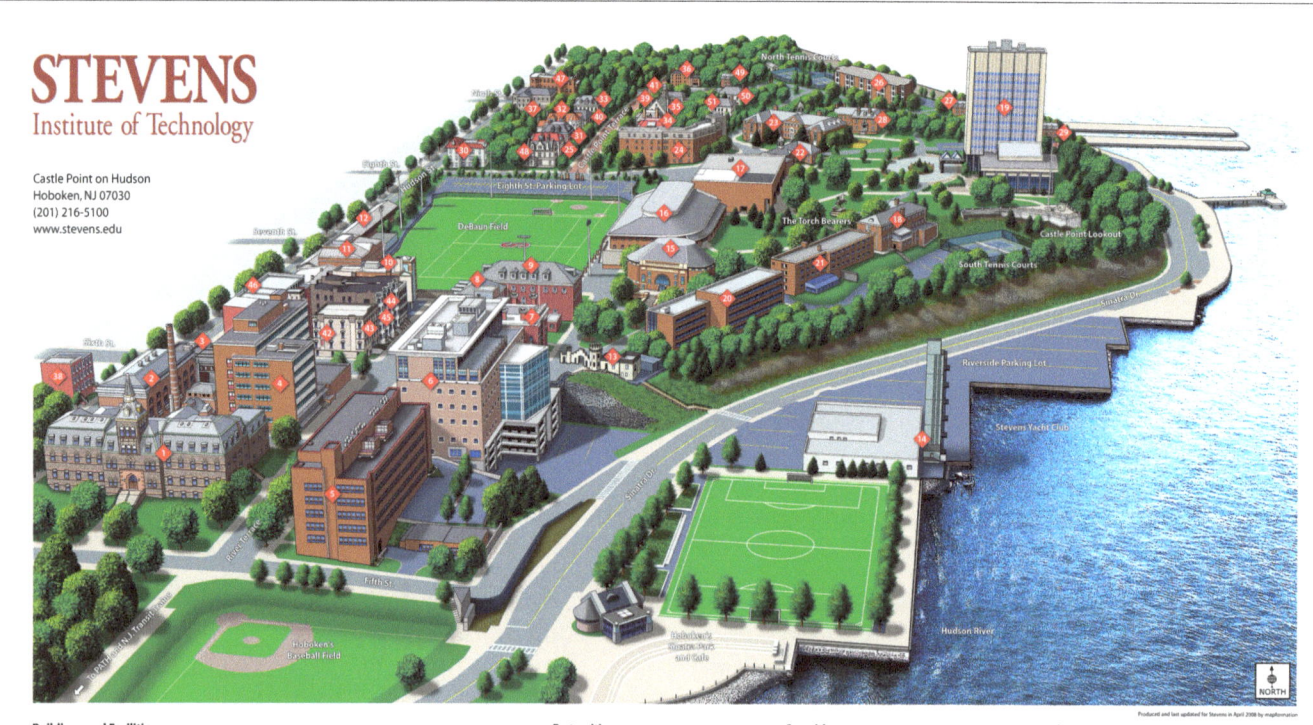

STEVENS
Institute of Technology

Castle Point on Hudson
Hoboken, NJ 07030
(201) 216-5100
www.stevens.edu

Buildings and Facilities:
1. Edwin A. Stevens Hall
2. Carnegie Laboratory
3. Lieb Building
4. Burchard Building
5. McLean Hall
6. Babbio Center
7-8-9. Morton-Pierce-Kidde Complex
10. Rocco Technology Center
11. Nicholl Environmental Laboratory
12. Davidson Laboratory
13. Gatehouse (Campus Police)

14. Griffith Building and
    Building Technology Tower
15. Walker Gymnasium
16. Schaefer Athletic
    and Recreation Center
17. Samuel C. Williams Library
    and Computer Center
18. Jacobus Student Center
19. Wesley J. Howe Center
    and Visitors Information Desk

27. Hoxie House
28. Alexander House
29. Colonial House

46. 607-614 Hudson St.
47. 901 Hudson St.
48. 800 Castle Point Terrace
49. 2 Ninth St.
50. Pollara House
51. Pond House

Fraternities:
30. Chi Phi - 801 Hudson St.
31. Chi Psi - 804 Castle Point Terrace
32. Sigma Nu - 806 Castle Point Terrace
33. Beta Theta Pi - 812 Castle Point Terrace
34. Theta Xi - 805 Castle Point Terrace
35. Delta Tau Delta - 809 Castle Point Terrace
36. Alpha Sigma Phi - 903 Castle Point Terrace
37. Phi Sigma Kappa - 837 Hudson St.
38. Sigma Phi Epsilon - 528-530 Hudson St.

Sororities:
39. Omicron Pi - 831 Castle Point Terrace
40. Delta Phi Epsilon - 808 Castle Point Terrace
41. Phi Sigma Sigma - 835 Castle Point Terrace

Residence Halls:
20. Davis Hall
21. Hayden Hall
22. Palmer Hall
23. Humphreys Hall
24. Jonas Hall
25. Lore-El Center
26. Castle Point Apartments

River Terrace Suites:
42. 600 River Terrace
43. 602 River Terrace
44. Gibb House - 604 River Terrace
45. 606 River Terrace

**Off-Campus Residence Halls
Not Shown:**
733 Jefferson Street
Avenue Apartments at 538 Washington Street

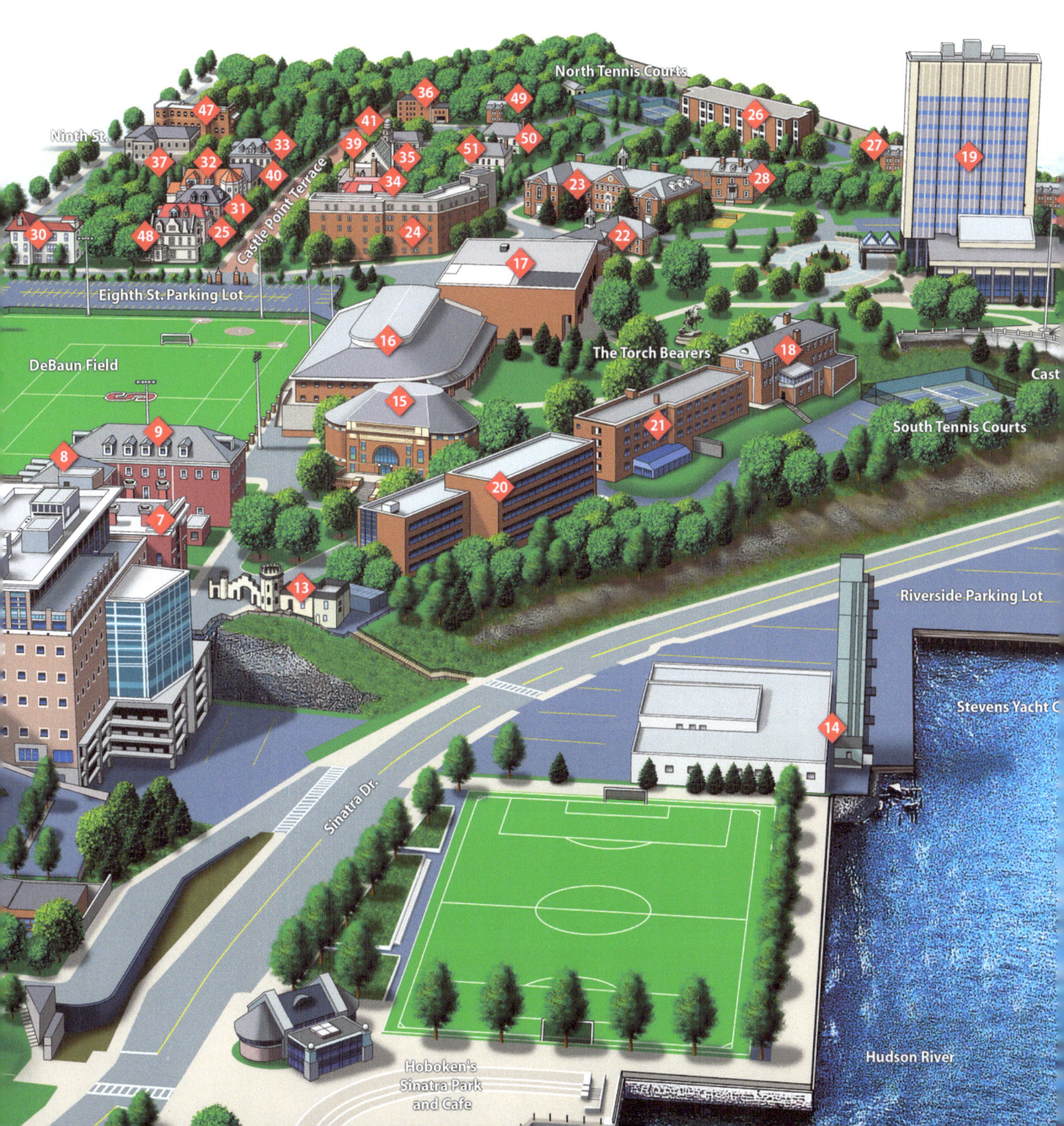

North Tennis Courts

Ninth St.

Castle Point Terrace

Eighth St. Parking Lot

DeBaun Field

The Torch Bearers

Cast

South Tennis Courts

Riverside Parking Lot

Stevens Yacht C

Sinatra Dr.

Hudson River

Hoboken's
Sinatra Park
and Cafe

47
36
49
26
37
32
33
41
39
35
51
50
27
19
40
34
23
28
31
25
24
22
30
48
17
18
16
15
21
9
20
8
7
13
14

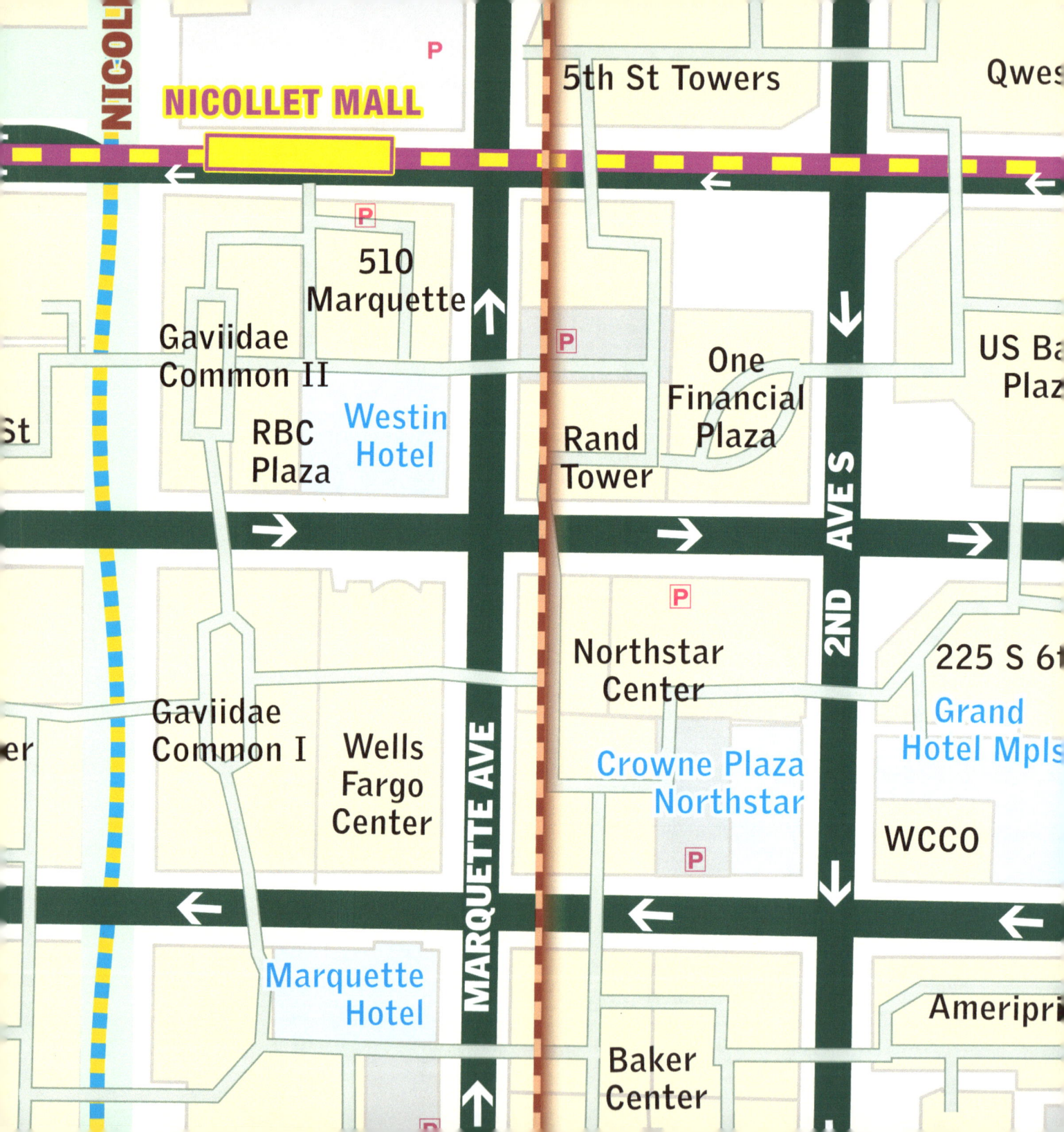

Nat Case, Hedberg Maps, Inc.

Nicollet Mall kiosk maps

Copyright ©2008 Hedberg Maps, Inc.

Software used: Adobe Illustrator, Adobe InDesign
More information: www.hedbergmaps.com

These kiosks are placed about one per block along Nicollet Mall, a pedestrian oasis in the heart of Minneapolis. The larger map serves as a general guide to downtown Minneapolis, while the Nicollet Mall Directory lists retail members of the Improvement District. Maps had to fit within fixed frames. The goal was to create easily editable and replaceable pieces to allow for regular updates.

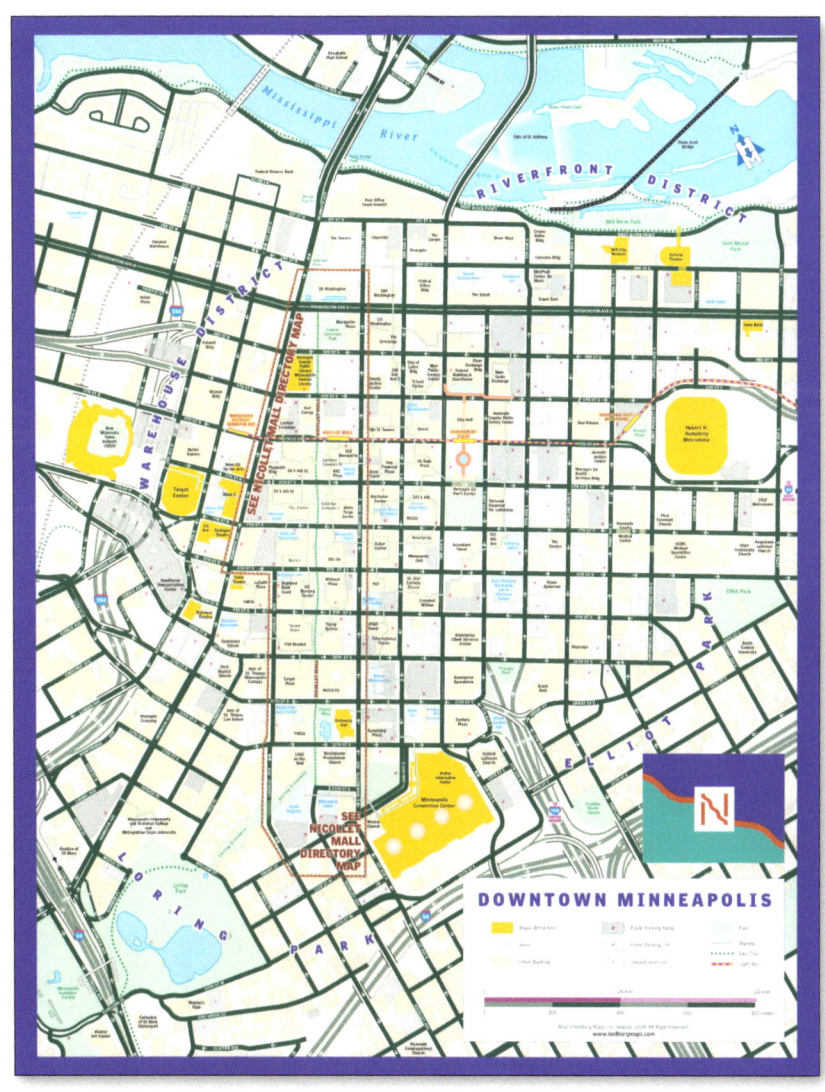

Claude Frank, Erin John LeFevre, Platts-McGraw-Hill

World Energy — Capacity & Consumption

Software Used: Adobe Illustrator CS3, ArcGIS Desktop 9.3, Adobe Photoshop CS3, Mapublisher 8.0

More information: www.maps.platts.com

Platts newly updated World Energy map presents the core components of the global energy market in vivid color. Explore the relationships between generation capacity, fuel types, and energy consumption. Discover the global interconnections of major shipping lanes, oil ports, refineries and LNG terminals overlaid on the most current geographic reference material available. Included also are key energy-related statistics presented in appealing charts and graphs.

Map Features:

- Countries colored by energy-consumed in quadrillion Btu (2005)
- Pie charts for every country sized by installed generation capacity (MW) and colored by primary fuel
- Oil & LNG shipping routes
- Major oil ports
- Oil refineries
- LNG terminals
- World countries with country name and country capital
- World time-zone reference
- Geographic reference grid lines

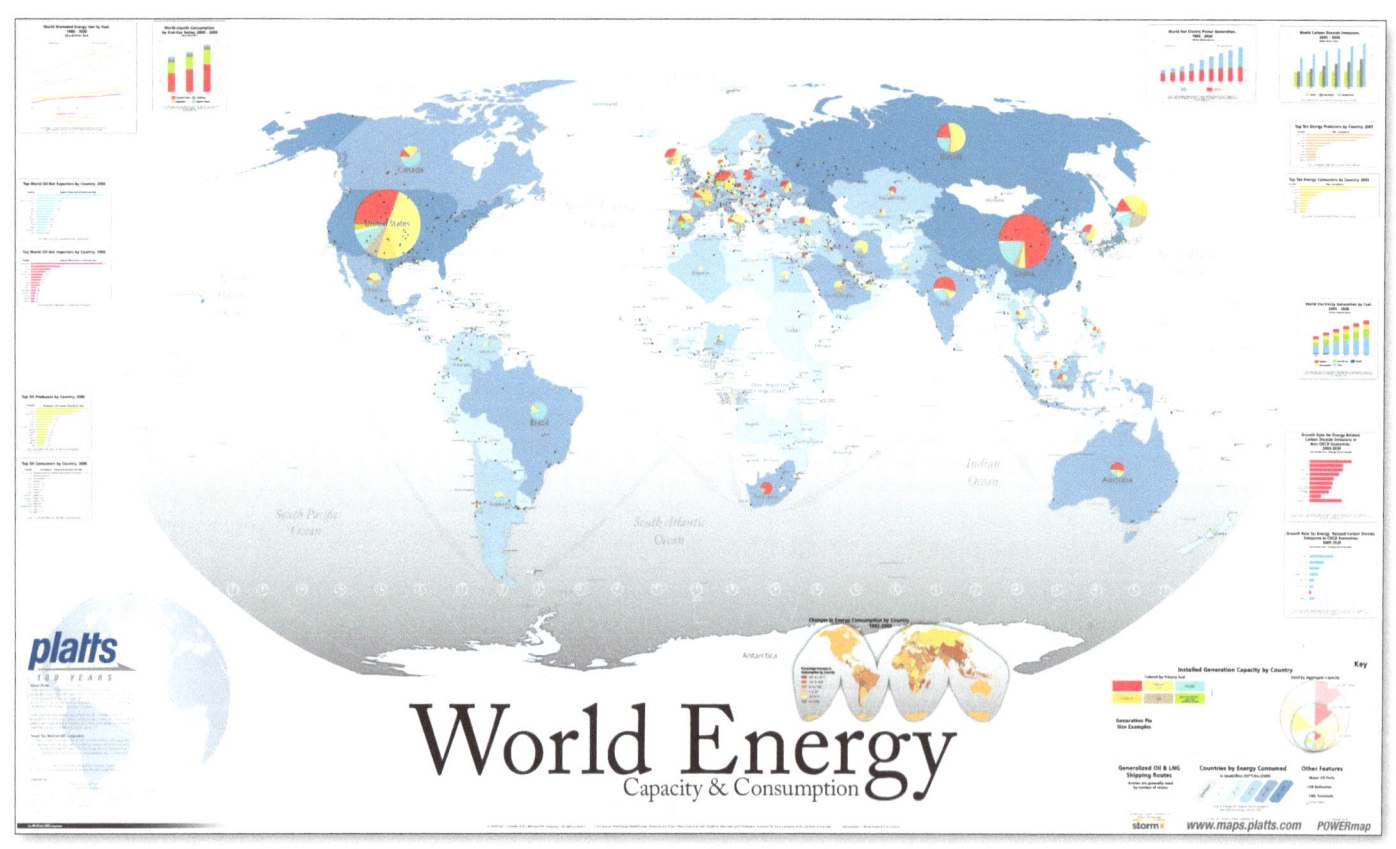

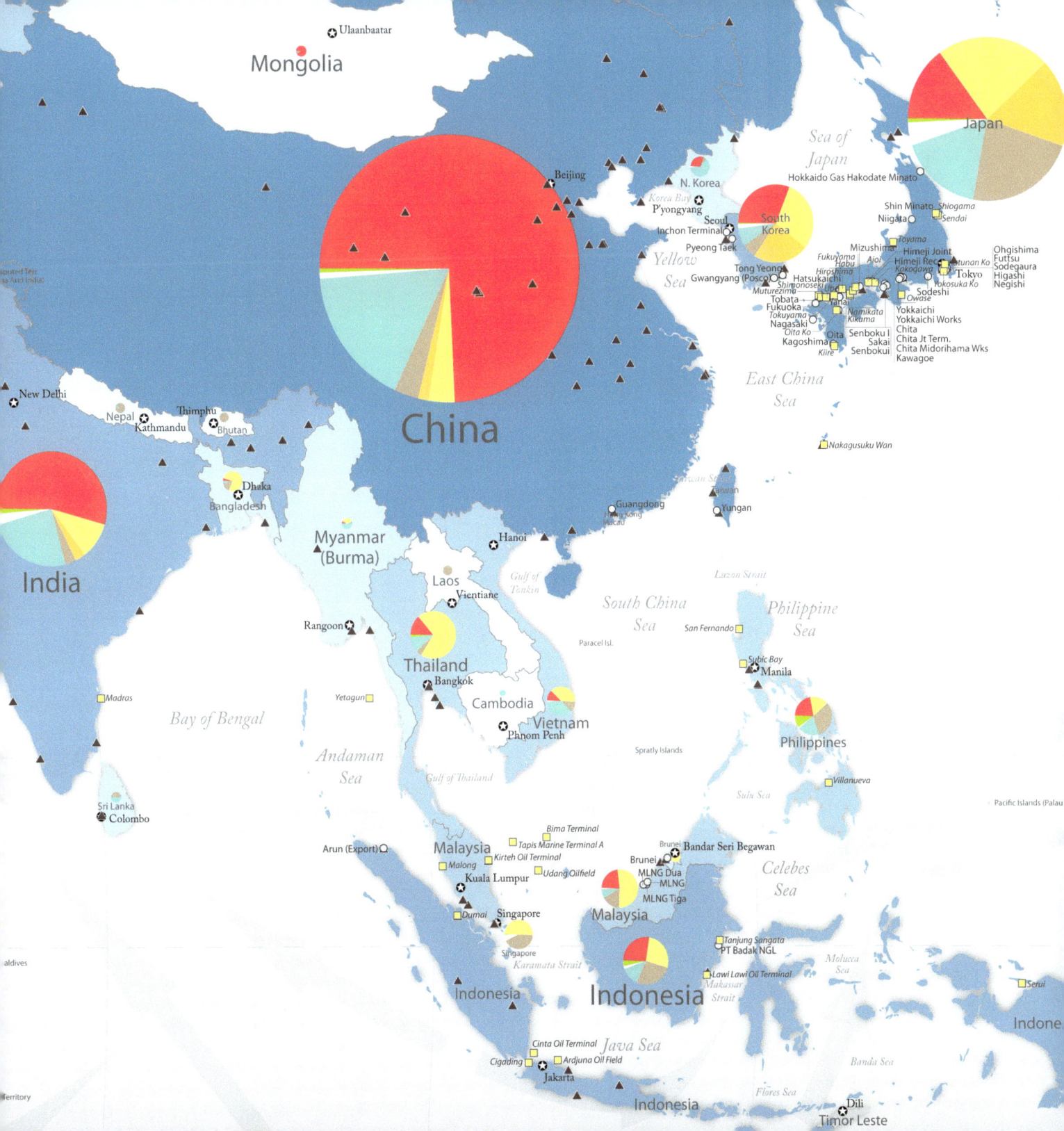

Ulaanbaatar

Mongolia

China

Beijing

N. Korea

P'yongyang
Seoul
Inchon Terminal
Pyeong Taek

South Korea

Sea of Japan

Japan

Hokkaido Gas Hakodate Minato

Shin Minato
Niigata
Shiogama
Sendai

Fukuyama
Habu
Ajoi
Mizushima
Himeji Joint
Himeji Rec.
Kokogawa
Hotunan Ko.

Ohgishima
Futtsu
Sodegaura
Higashi
Negishi

Hatsukaichi
Muturezima
Hiroshima
Shimonoseki Ube
Tobata
Fukuoka
Tokuyama
Nagasaki
Oita Ko
Kagoshima
Kiire

Yellow Sea

Tong Yeong
Gwangyang (Posco)

Toyama

Yokosuka Ko
Tokyo

Sodeshi
Owase

Namikata
Kikuma
Oita
Senboku I
Senbokui
Sakai

Yokkaichi
Yokkaichi Works
Chita
Chita Jt Term.
Chita Midorihama Wks
Kawagoe

East China Sea

Nakagusuku Wan

New Delhi

Nepal
Kathmandu

Thimphu
Bhutan

Dhaka
Bangladesh

Myanmar (Burma)

India

Laos
Vientiane

Thailand

Bangkok

Hanoi

Guangdong
Macau

Yungan

South China Sea

Philippine Sea

Luzon Strait

San Fernando

Subic Bay
Manila

Rangoon

Yetagun

Cambodia

Phnom Penh

Vietnam

Paracel Isl.

Spratly Islands

Madras

Bay of Bengal

Andaman Sea

Gulf of Thailand

Philippines

Sulu Sea

Villanueva

Pacific Islands (Palau

Sri Lanka
Colombo

Bima Terminal

Tapis Marine Terminal A

Arun (Export)

Malaysia

Malong

Kirteh Oil Terminal

Udang Oilfield

Brunei
Bandar Seri Begawan

MLNG Dua
MLNG
MLNG Tiga

Brunei

Celebes Sea

Kuala Lumpur

Dumai

Singapore

Singapore

Indonesia

Malaysia

Indonesia

Karamata Strait

Indonesia

Tanjung Sangata
PT Badak NGL

Lawi Lawi Oil Terminal
Makassar
Strait

Moluccas Sea

Serui

aldives

Cinta Oil Terminal

Cigading
Jakarta

Ardjuna Oil Field

Java Sea

Banda Sea

Flores Sea

Indone

Indonesia

Dili
Timor Leste

Territory

W E N D A K E

toanche

Penetanguishene Peninsula

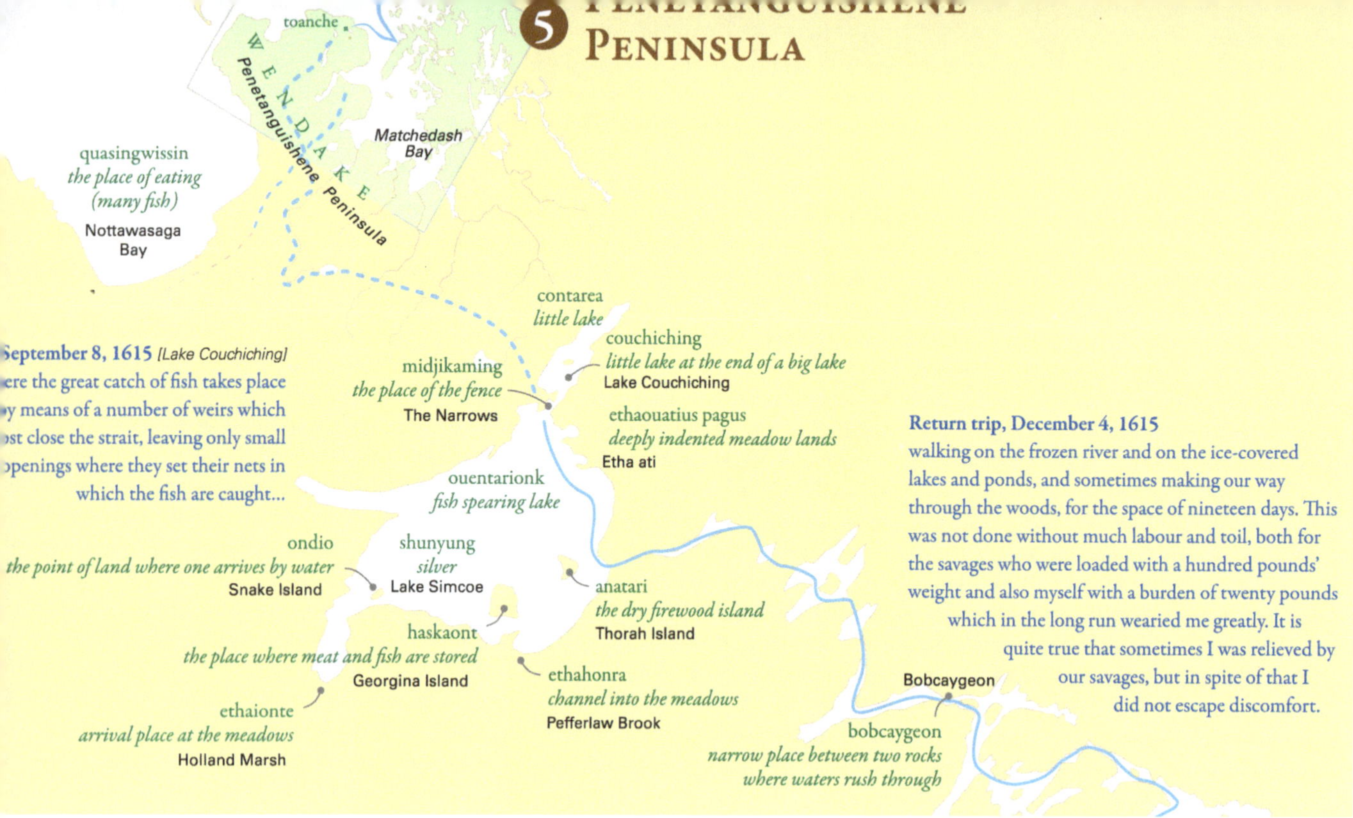

Matchedash
Bay

quasingwissin
*the place of eating
(many fish)*
Nottawasaga
Bay

contarea
little lake

couchiching
little lake at the end of a big lake
Lake Couchiching

midjikaming
the place of the fence
The Narrows

ethaouatius pagus
deeply indented meadow lands
Etha ati

September 8, 1615 *[Lake Couchiching]*
here the great catch of fish takes place
by means of a number of weirs which
most close the strait, leaving only small
openings where they set their nets in
which the fish are caught...

ouentarionk
fish spearing lake

ondio
the point of land where one arrives by water
Snake Island

shunyung
silver
Lake Simcoe

anatari
the dry firewood island
Thorah Island

haskaont
the place where meat and fish are stored
Georgina Island

ethahonra
channel into the meadows
Pefferlaw Brook

ethaionte
arrival place at the meadows
Holland Marsh

bobcaygeon
*narrow place between two rocks
where waters rush through*

Bobcaygeon

Return trip, December 4, 1615
walking on the frozen river and on the ice-covered
lakes and ponds, and sometimes making our way
through the woods, for the space of nineteen days. This
was not done without much labour and toil, both for
the savages who were loaded with a hundred pounds'
weight and also myself with a burden of twenty pounds
which in the long run wearied me greatly. It is
quite true that sometimes I was relieved by
our savages, but in spite of that I
did not escape discomfort.

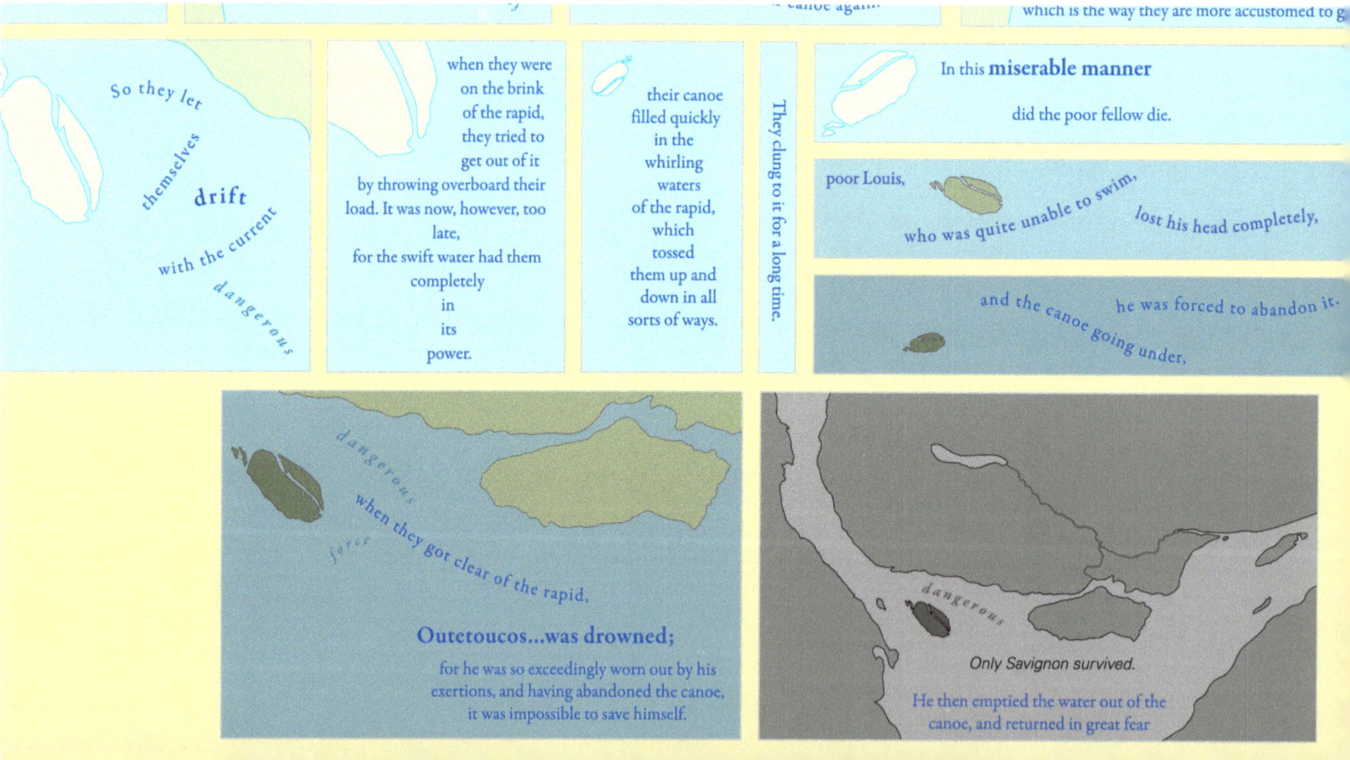

---

canoe again...

which is the way they are more accustomed to g

So they let
themselves
drift
with the current
dangerous

when they were
on the brink
of the rapid,
they tried to
get out of it
by throwing overboard their
load. It was now, however, too
late,
for the swift water had them
completely
in
its
power.

their canoe
filled quickly
in the
whirling
waters
of the rapid,
which
tossed
them up and
down in all
sorts of ways.

They clung to it for a long time.

In this **miserable manner**

did the poor fellow die.

poor Louis,
who was quite unable to swim,

lost his head completely,

and the canoe going under,
he was forced to abandon it.

dangerous
when they got clear of the rapid,
force

Outetoucos...was drowned;

for he was so exceedingly worn out by his
exertions, and having abandoned the canoe,
it was impossible to save himself.

dangerous

Only Savignon survived.

He then emptied the water out of the
canoe, and returned in great fear.

Michael James Hermann, University of Maine
Margaret Wickens Pearce, Ohio University
Raymond Pelletier, University of Maine, University of Maine Canadian-American Center

They Would Not take Me There: People, Places and Stories from Champlain's Travels in Canada, 1603–1616

Copyright: © University of Maine which agrees to this publication use.

Software Used: ESRI ArcMap, Adobe Illustrator CS3, Adobe Photoshop CS
More information:
www.umaine.edu/canam/cartography/Champlain.html

In 2008 cartographers Michael Hermann (University of Maine) and Margaret Pearce (Ohio University) collaborated on a project to illustrate the travel journals of Samuel de Champlain in the 1600s. Within the context of a larger map (39 x 59 inches), a series of narrative panels were developed to convey more than simply showing where Champlain was; they were designed to bring the reader into the storied landscape by conveying elements of isolation, seasonality, danger, despair, death, hope, and survival. Champlain's voice is from his journals (typeset in blue), a hypothetical Native voice responds (in green), and the cartographers voice (in black) moves the story along. The map is bilingual with French on one side and English on the other.

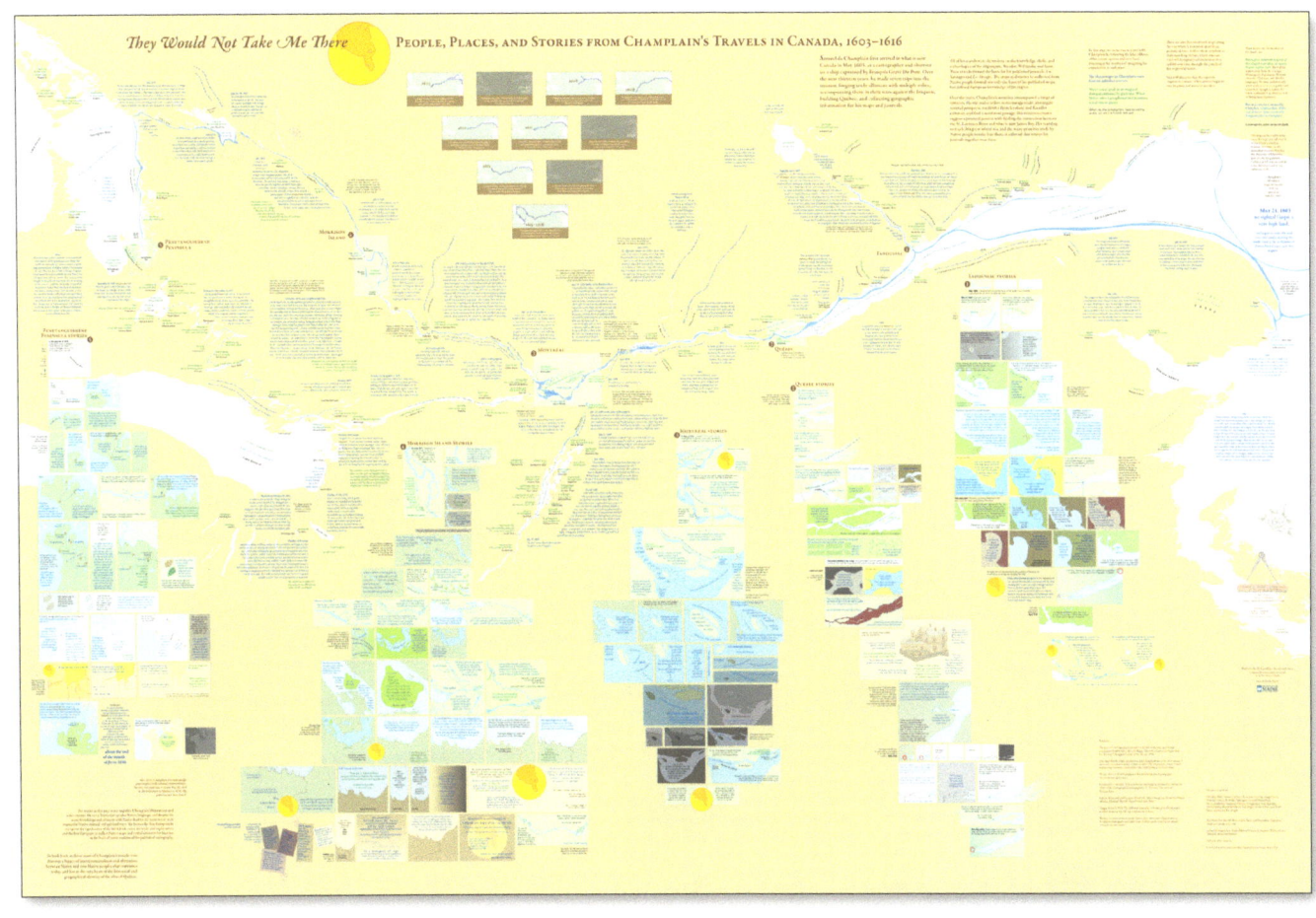

Daniel P. Huffman

Visualizing Airfare

Copyright: 2008, Daniel P. Huffman

Software Used: ArcGIS 9.2 and Adobe Illustrator CS3

By the conventions I have learned in school, this map should not have been made. Airfare is not a continuous phenomenon - we can only fly to specific place. Thus, interpolating and threading isolines is not the best choice. However, I believe that the result is much more visually striking than a traditional choice, such as proportional symbols. The light and shadow effect and the isolines emphasize how, even within a region, major fluctuations can occur in air travel cost.

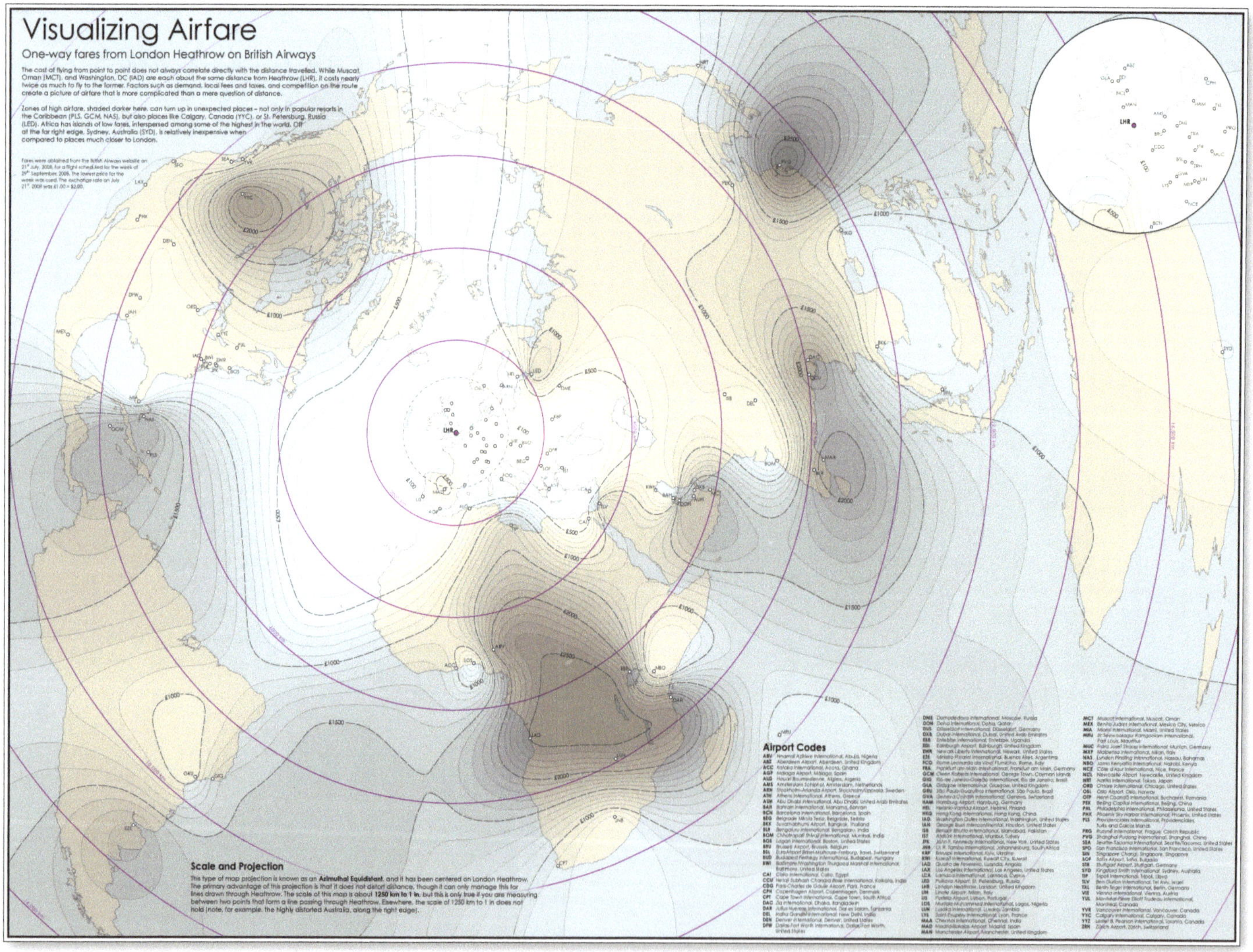

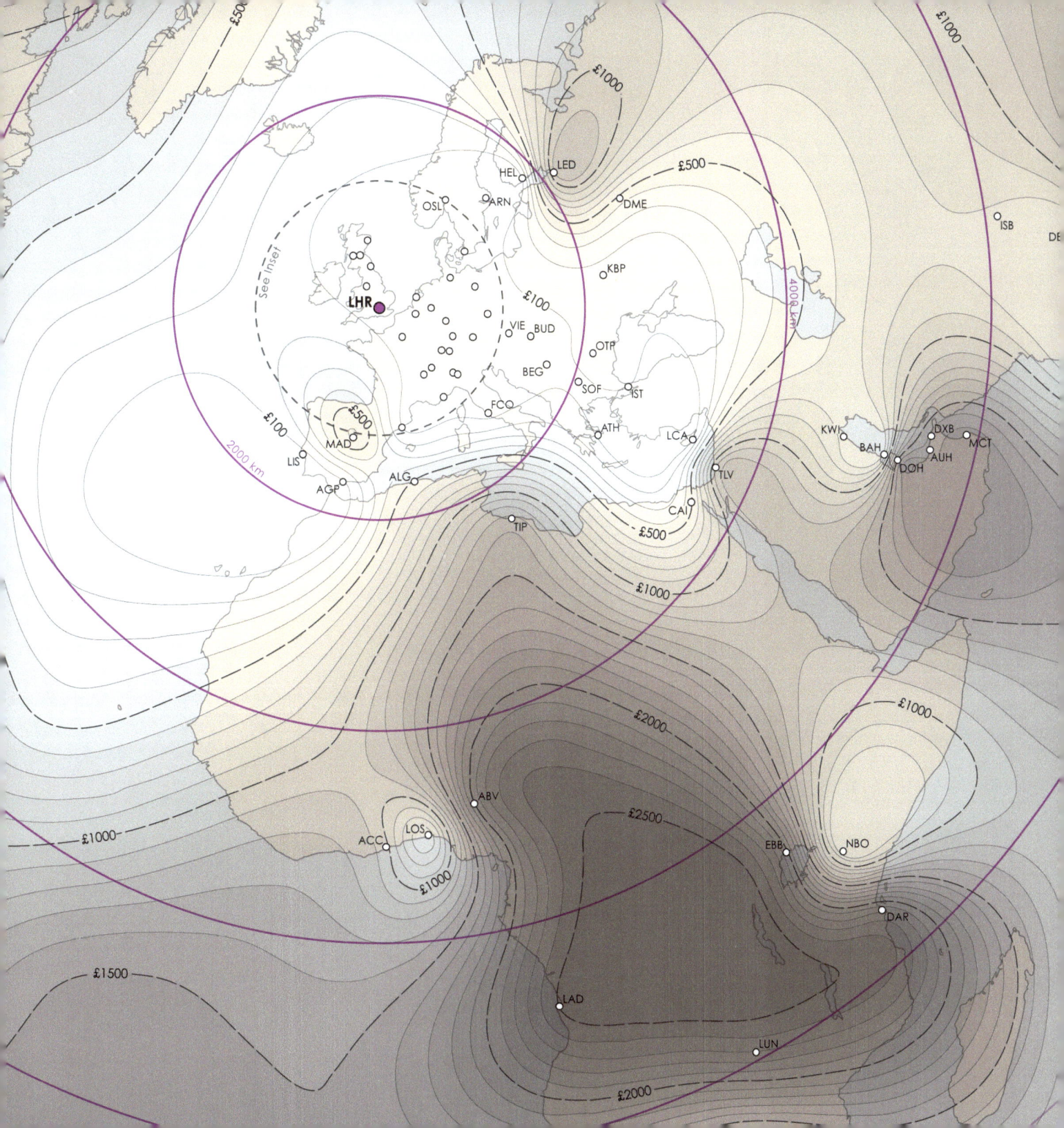

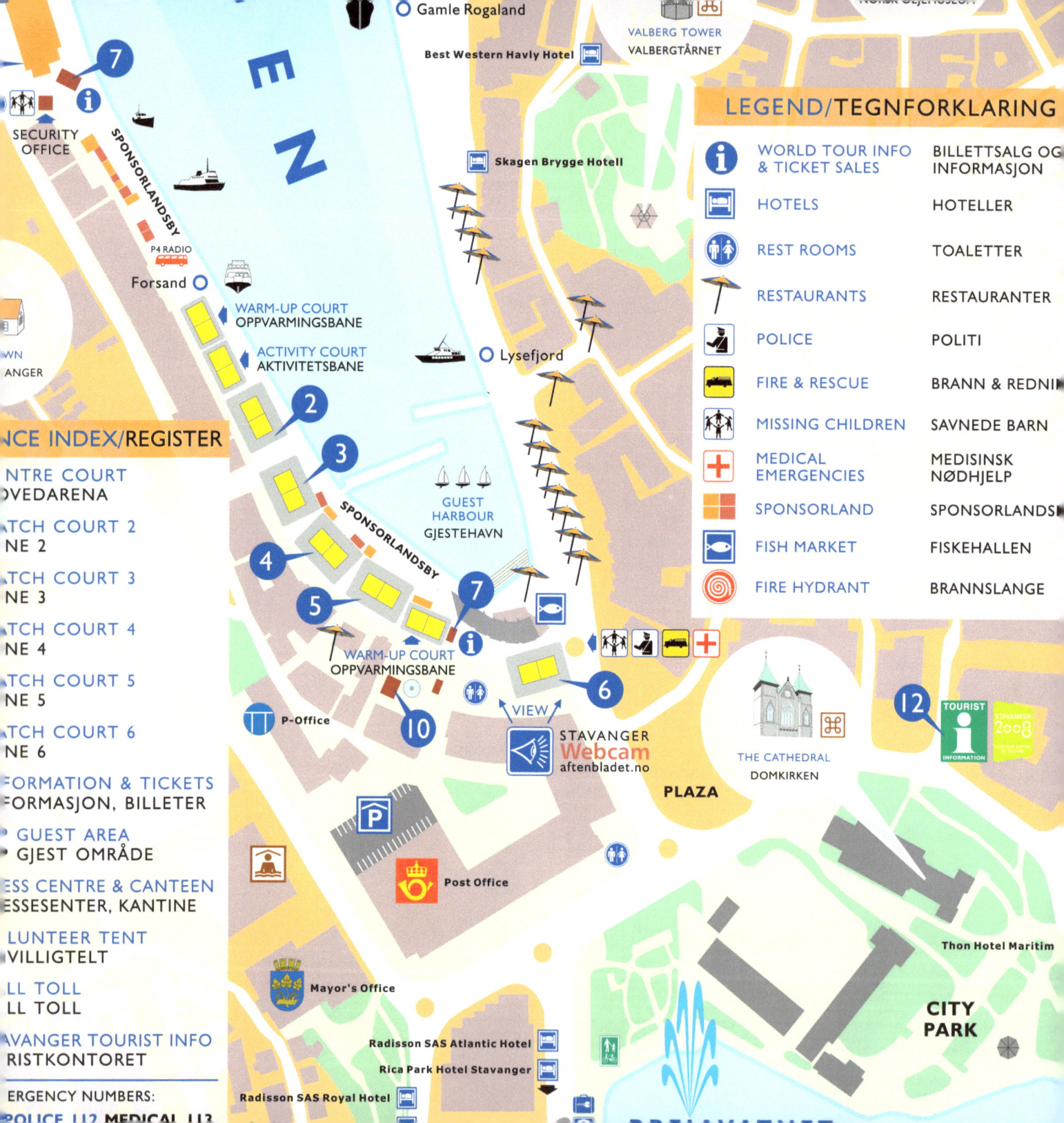

LEGEND/TEGNFORKLARING

WORLD TOUR INFO & TICKET SALES	BILLETTSALG OG INFORMASJON
HOTELS	HOTELLER
REST ROOMS	TOALETTER
RESTAURANTS	RESTAURANTER
POLICE	POLITI
FIRE & RESCUE	BRANN & REDNI...
MISSING CHILDREN	SAVNEDE BARN
MEDICAL EMERGENCIES	MEDISINSK NØDHJELP
SPONSORLAND	SPONSORLANDS...
FISH MARKET	FISKEHALLEN
FIRE HYDRANT	BRANNSLANGE

SECURITY OFFICE

SPONSORLANDSBY

P4 RADIO

Forsand

WARM-UP COURT
OPPVARMINGSBANE

ACTIVITY COURT
AKTIVITETSBANE

2

3

SPONSORLANDSBY

4

5

7

WARM-UP COURT
OPPVARMINGSBANE

P-Office

10

VIEW

STAVANGER
Webcam
aftenbladet.no

6

PLAZA

THE CATHEDRAL
DOMKIRKEN

12

TOURIST
INFORMATION

STAVANGER
2008

Gamle Rogaland

VALBERG TOWER
VALBERGTÅRNET

Best Western Havly Hotel

Skagen Brygge Hotell

Lysefjord

GUEST HARBOUR
GJESTEHAVN

Post Office

Mayor's Office

Thon Hotel Maritim

CITY PARK

Radisson SAS Atlantic Hotel

Rica Park Hotel Stavanger

Radisson SAS Royal Hotel

...ANGER

...EN

...NCE INDEX/REGISTER

...NTRE COURT
...OVEDARENA

...TCH COURT 2
...NE 2

...TCH COURT 3
...NE 3

...TCH COURT 4
...NE 4

...TCH COURT 5
...NE 5

...TCH COURT 6
...NE 6

...FORMATION & TICKETS
...FORMASJON, BILLETER

...GUEST AREA
...GJEST OMRÅDE

...ESS CENTRE & CANTEEN
...ESSESENTER, KANTINE

...LUNTEER TENT
...VILLIGTELT

...LL TOLL
...LL TOLL

...AVANGER TOURIST INFO
...RISTKONTORET

...ERGENCY NUMBERS:
...OLICE 112 MEDICAL 113

Kevin Paul Scarrott, Stavanger Guide Maps Norway

Swatch Fivb Beach Volley World Tour 2008

More information: www.stavanger-guide.no/worldtourstavanger/

Copyright: 2008 © STAVANGER GUIDE MAPS NORWAY

Software Used: CorelDraw, Adobe Photoshop, Adobe Acrobat, Adobe Dreamweaver

Annual festivals and sports events usually generate the need for an informative map. This particular map has been designed to facilitate the general public and officials in locating the various match courts and other features of significance. Although simple in composition, the map is extremely functional and has a straightforward and comprehendible content and propose. Simplicity in mapmaking is not easily attained. Here the focus is primarily on thoroughfare and public safety.   Uses:- Web- Poster- Program- Pocket Map- Newspaper

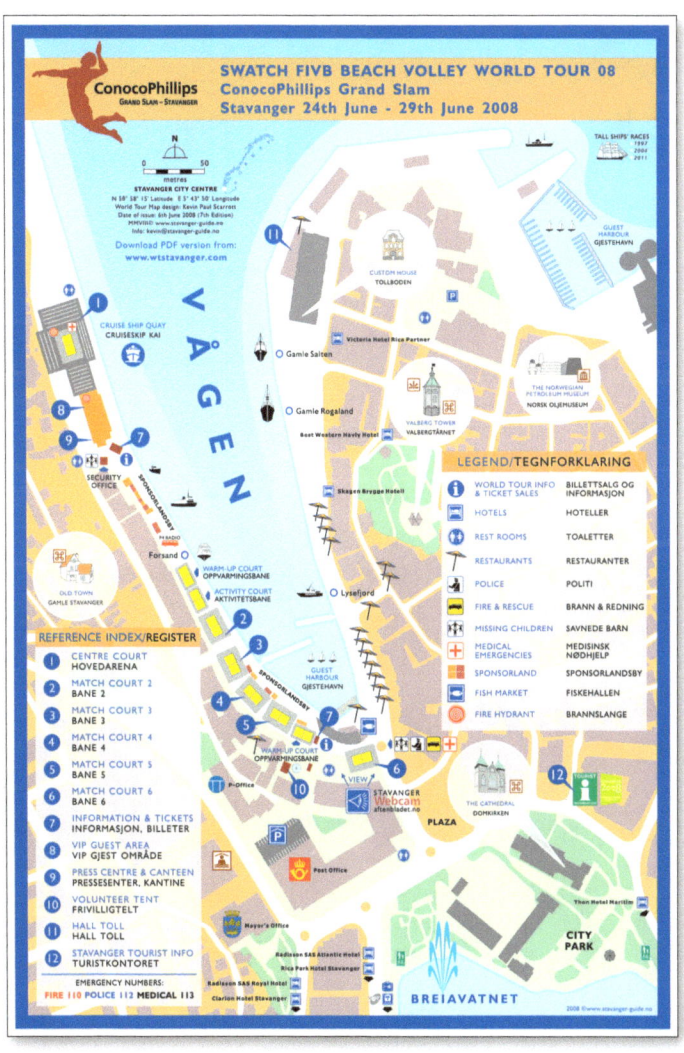

Michael Scisco, BioGeoCreations

Colorado Fourteeners

Copyright: © 2009 BioGeoCreations

Software Used: ArcView 9.1, Adobe Illustrator, Adobe Photoshop

This decorative map shows the location and elevation of all 14,000+ ft. mountain peaks in the State of Colorado. The poster also employs graphs to show comparative elevations and what peaks are located in which mountain ranges.

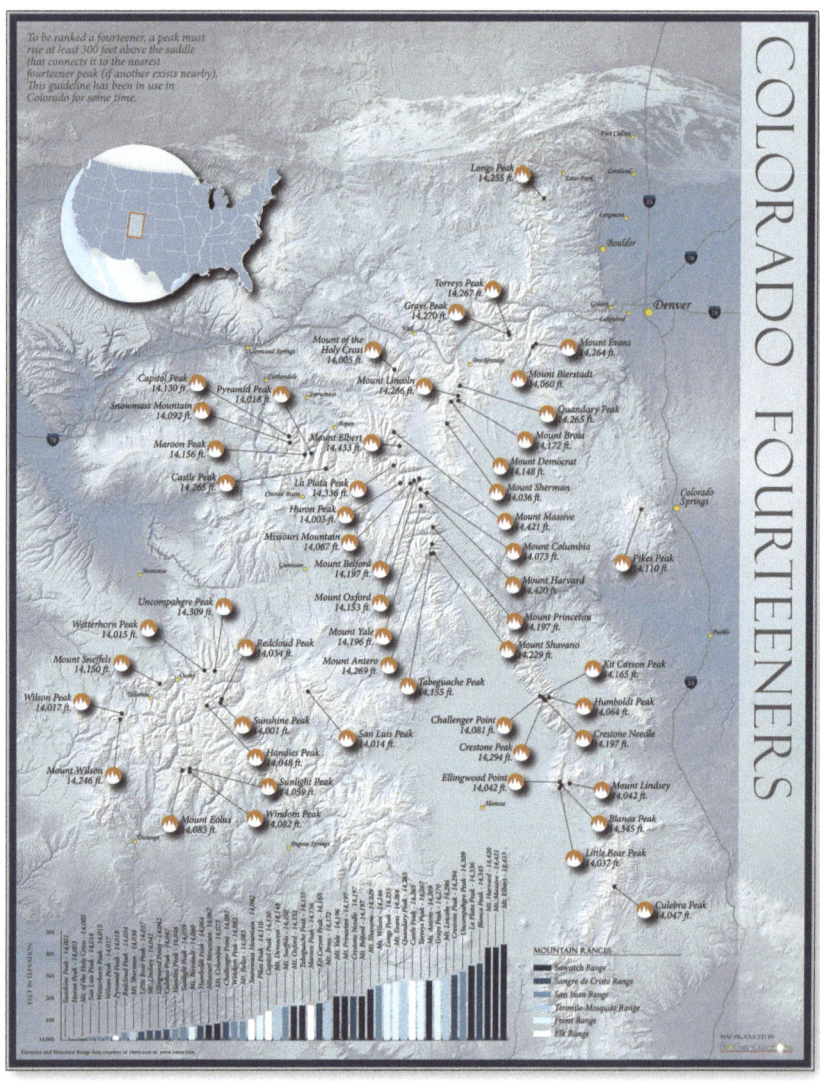

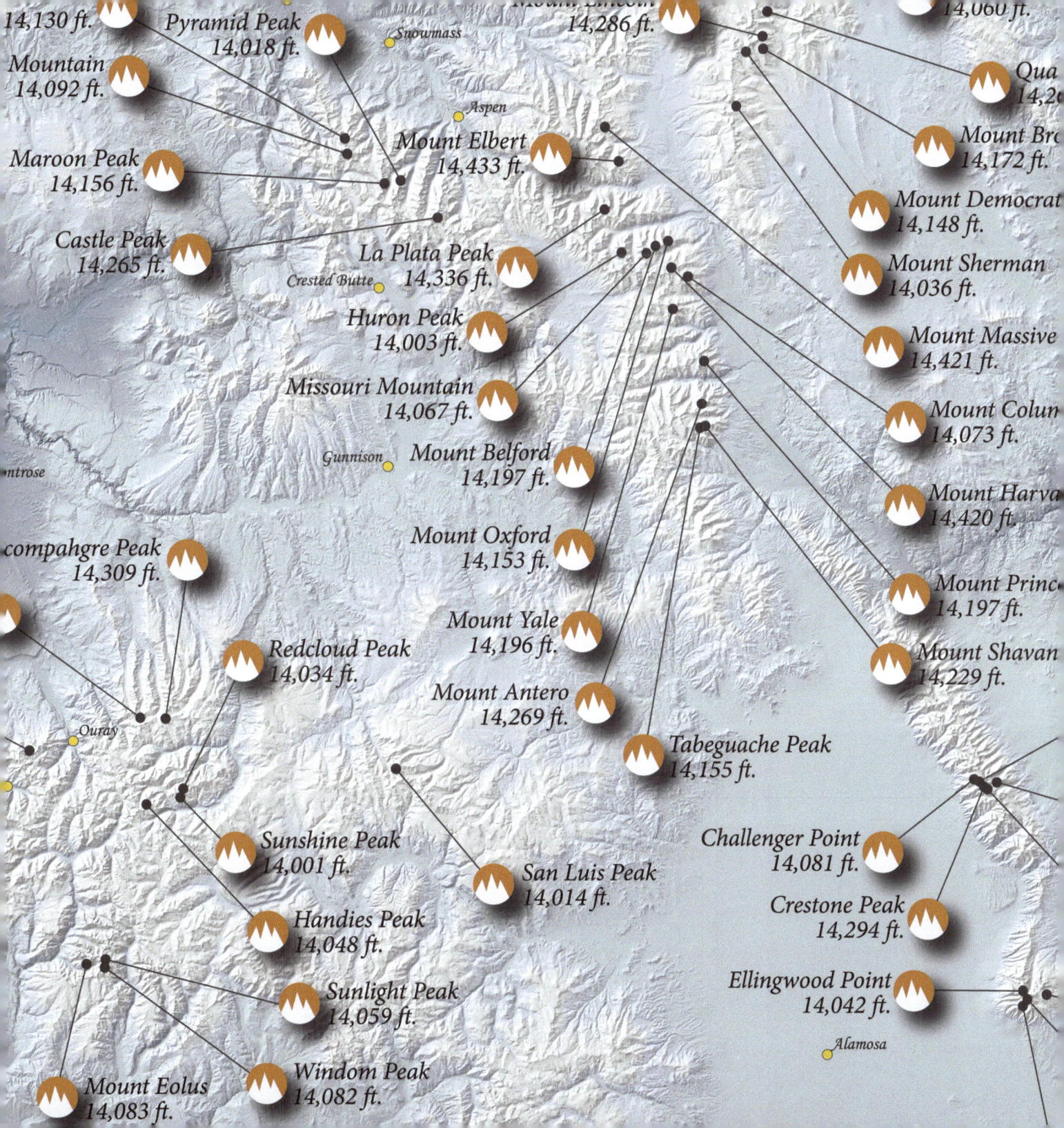

14,130 ft.

Pyramid Peak
14,018 ft.

Snowmass

14,286 ft.

14,060 ft.

Mountain
14,092 ft.

Aspen

Qua
14,2

Mount Br
14,172 ft.

Maroon Peak
14,156 ft.

Mount Elbert
14,433 ft.

Mount Democrat
14,148 ft.

Castle Peak
14,265 ft.

La Plata Peak
14,336 ft.

Crested Butte

Mount Sherman
14,036 ft.

Huron Peak
14,003 ft.

Mount Massive
14,421 ft.

Missouri Mountain
14,067 ft.

Mount Colun
14,073 ft.

Gunnison

Mount Belford
14,197 ft.

Mount Harva
14,420 ft.

ntrose

compahgre Peak
14,309 ft.

Mount Oxford
14,153 ft.

Mount Princ
14,197 ft.

Redcloud Peak
14,034 ft.

Mount Yale
14,196 ft.

Mount Shavan
14,229 ft.

Mount Antero
14,269 ft.

Ouray

Tabeguache Peak
14,155 ft.

Sunshine Peak
14,001 ft.

Challenger Point
14,081 ft.

San Luis Peak
14,014 ft.

Crestone Peak
14,294 ft.

Handies Peak
14,048 ft.

Ellingwood Point
14,042 ft.

Sunlight Peak
14,059 ft.

Alamosa

Mount Eolus
14,083 ft.

Windom Peak
14,082 ft.

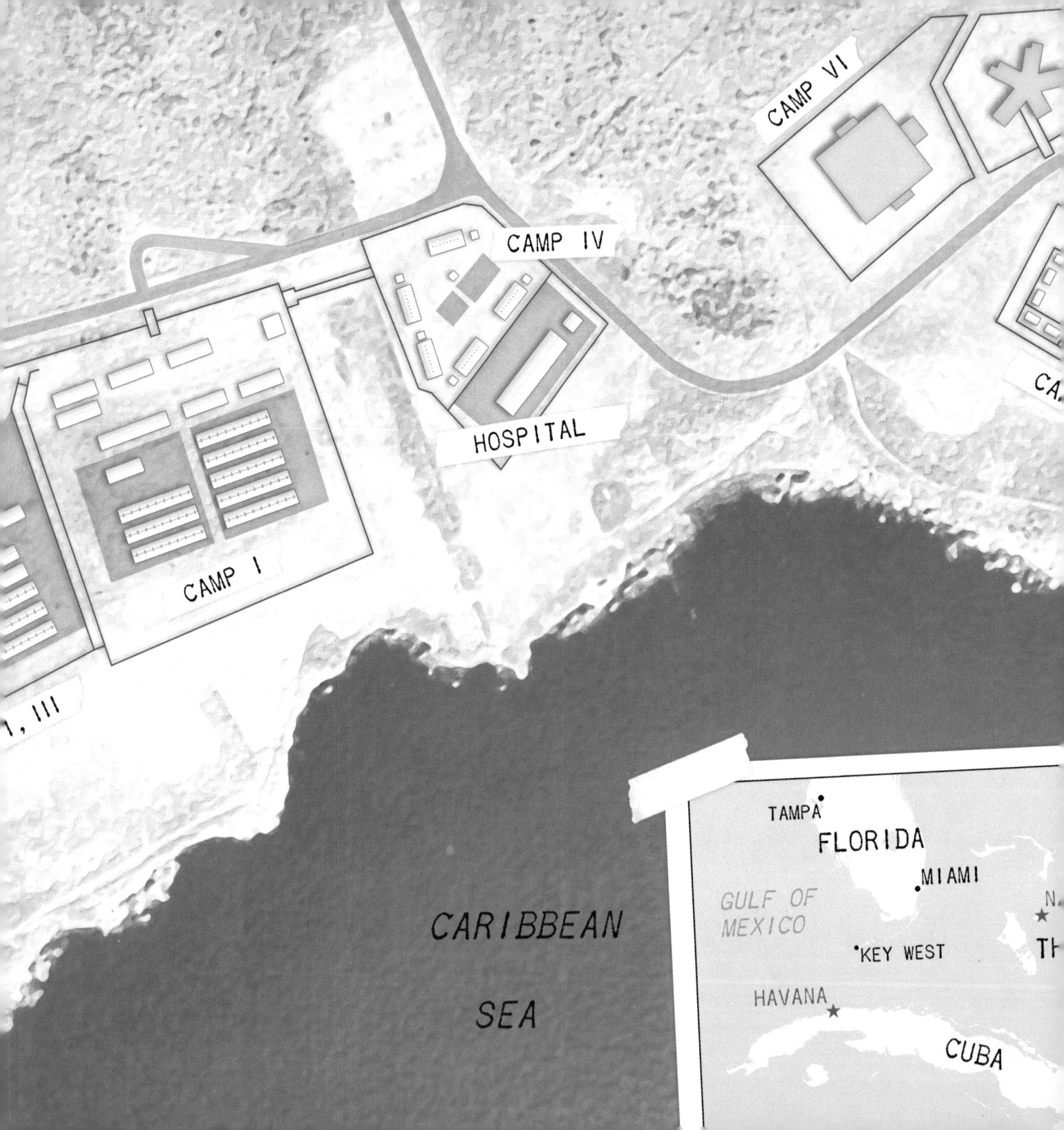

Nick Springer, Springer Cartographics LLC

Camp Delta, Guantanamo Bay
Copyright © 2008 HarperCollins Publishing

Software used: Adobe Illustrator, Adobe Photoshop
More information: www.springercartographics.com

Published in "Inside Gitmo: The True Story Behind the Myths of Guantanamo Bay" by Gordon Cucullu. I designed this to look like an annotated image from a CIA dossier. I scanned pieces of masking tape to use for the labels and a typeface that mimic a Leroy lettering machine.

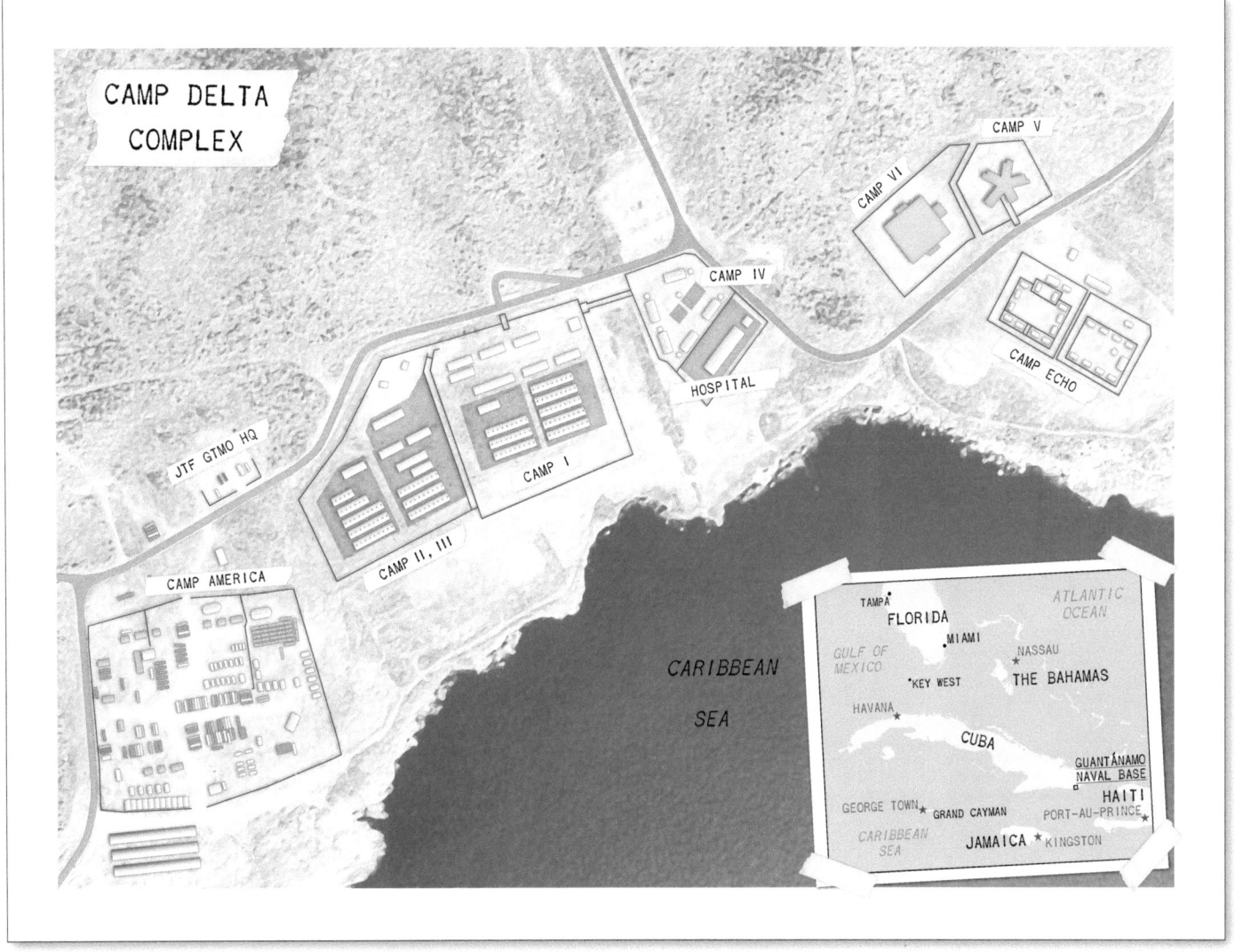

Nathaniel Vaughn Kelso, The Washington Post

Proposed Purple Line: Route and stations

Copyright © 2008 by The Washington Post

Software used: Adobe Illustrator CS3 and Vectorworks 12.5 with Azimuth plugin.

More information: washingtonpost.com

The Purple Line has been on the planning horizon for many years in Maryland but it really got moving in 2008. The route twists and turns thru existing urban landscape and our readers want to know the specifics which allowed for a larger reference map than our usual locator service. The state releases PDFs of the alignment posters showing their latest proposals. Once those are stitched together in Illustrator I export to DXW format and register and tweak to fit with our Washington DC basemap in VectorWorks. The final labeling and design is done back in Illustrator.

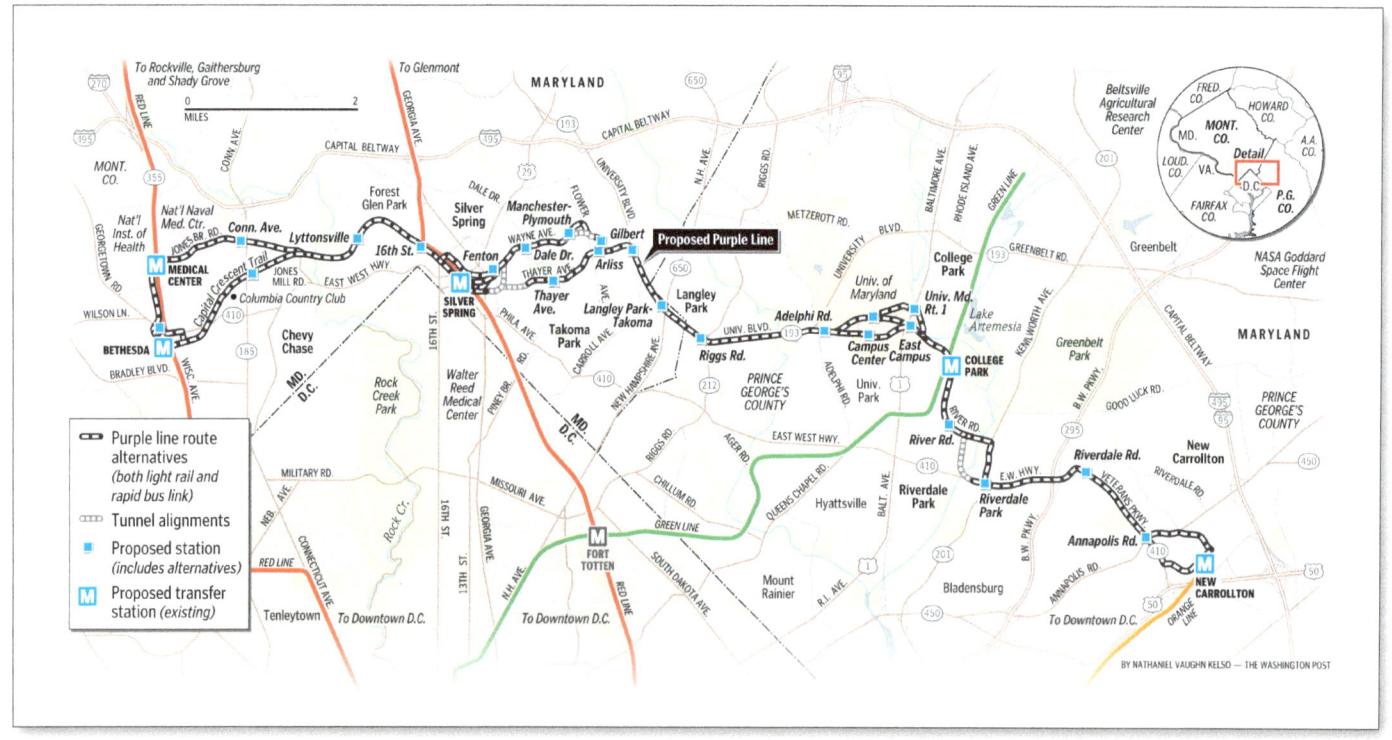

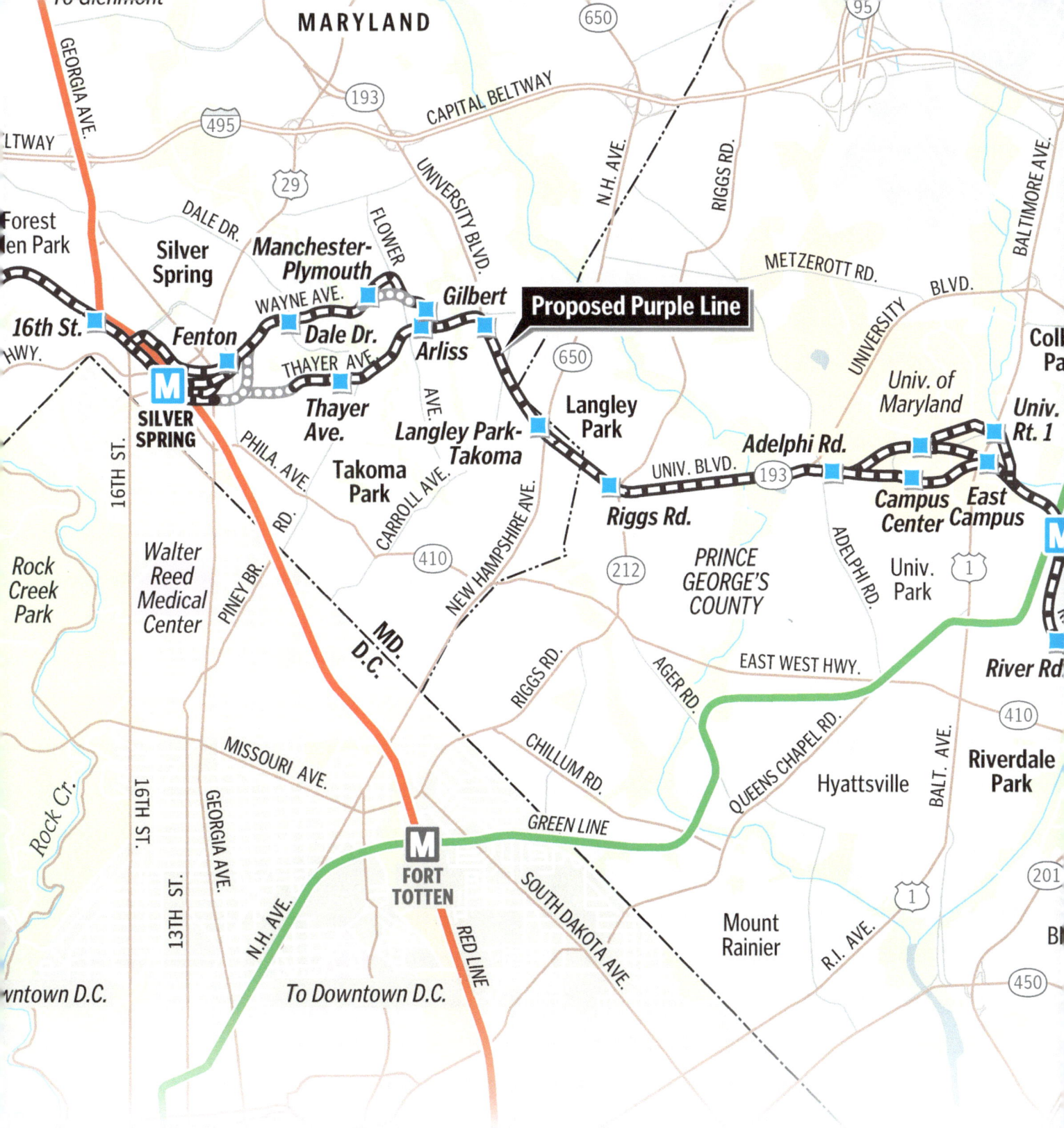

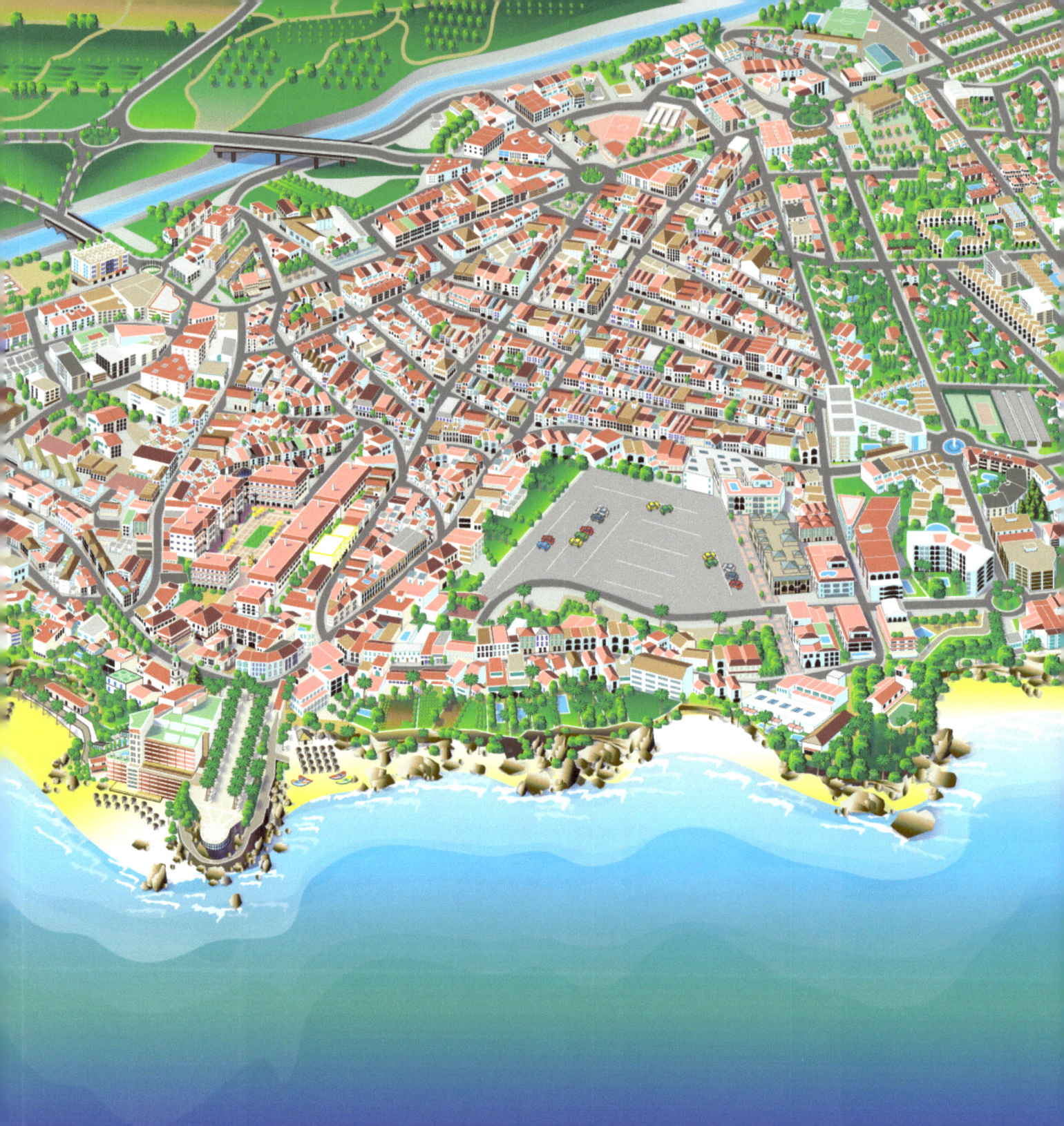

Michael Karpovage, Mapformation, LLC

Nerja, Malaga, Spain

More information: www.mapformation.com/portfolio/tourism/nerja3D.htm

Copyright: 2008 3D-Destinations.com
Software Used: Adobe Illustrator CS3

3D-Destinations.com hired Mapformation to develop a 3D perspective illustration of Nerja, Malaga, Spain in effort to promote it as a destination for potential visitors, businesses and residents. Map illustrator Michael Karpovage used available online aerial and birds-eye-view photographic resources as well as ground photos submitted by client in order to render this map. The illustration was then turned into an interactive map on the client website.

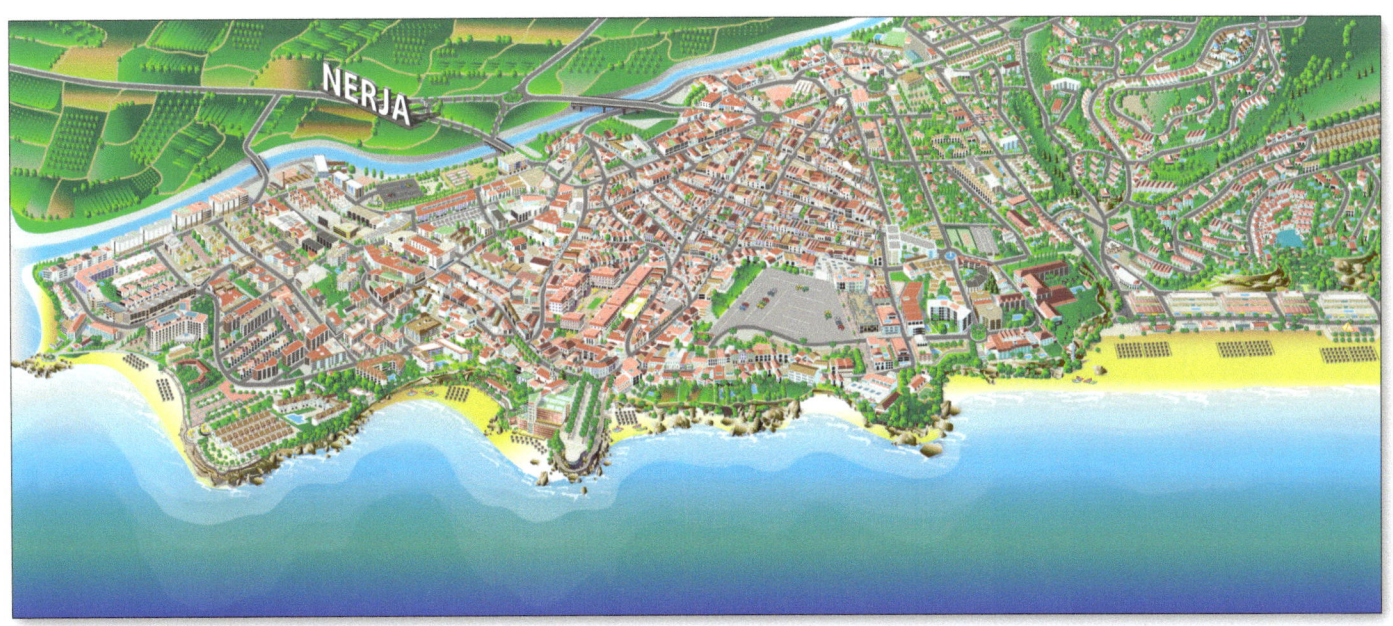

Nat Case, Hedberg Maps

Les collèges et les universités du Canada: Carte de référence / Colleges and Universities of Canada: Reference Map

Copyright ©Her Majesty the Queen in Right of Canada 2008

Software used: Adobe Illustrator using MaPublisher, Adobe InDesign, FileMaker

More information: www.hedbergmaps.com

The map was designed to help explain Canada's higher education opportunities to foreign potential students. It shows higher education institutions in Canada approved to accept foreign students through Citizenship and Immigration Canada. The reverse side includes client-supplied graphics describing the provincial systems of education, and a detailed index of institutions with contact and degree-granting information. Base mapping included public data from Natural Resources Canada.

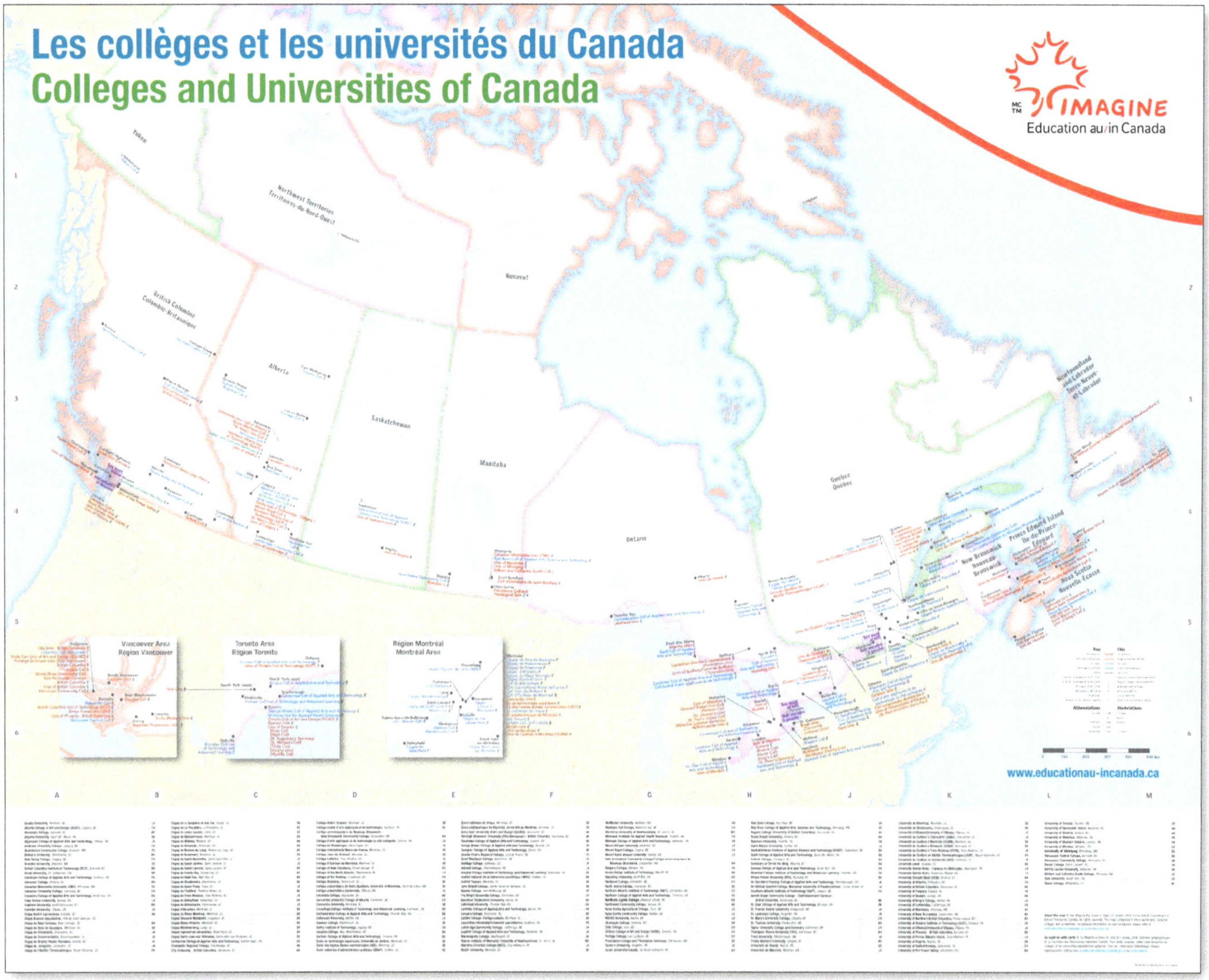

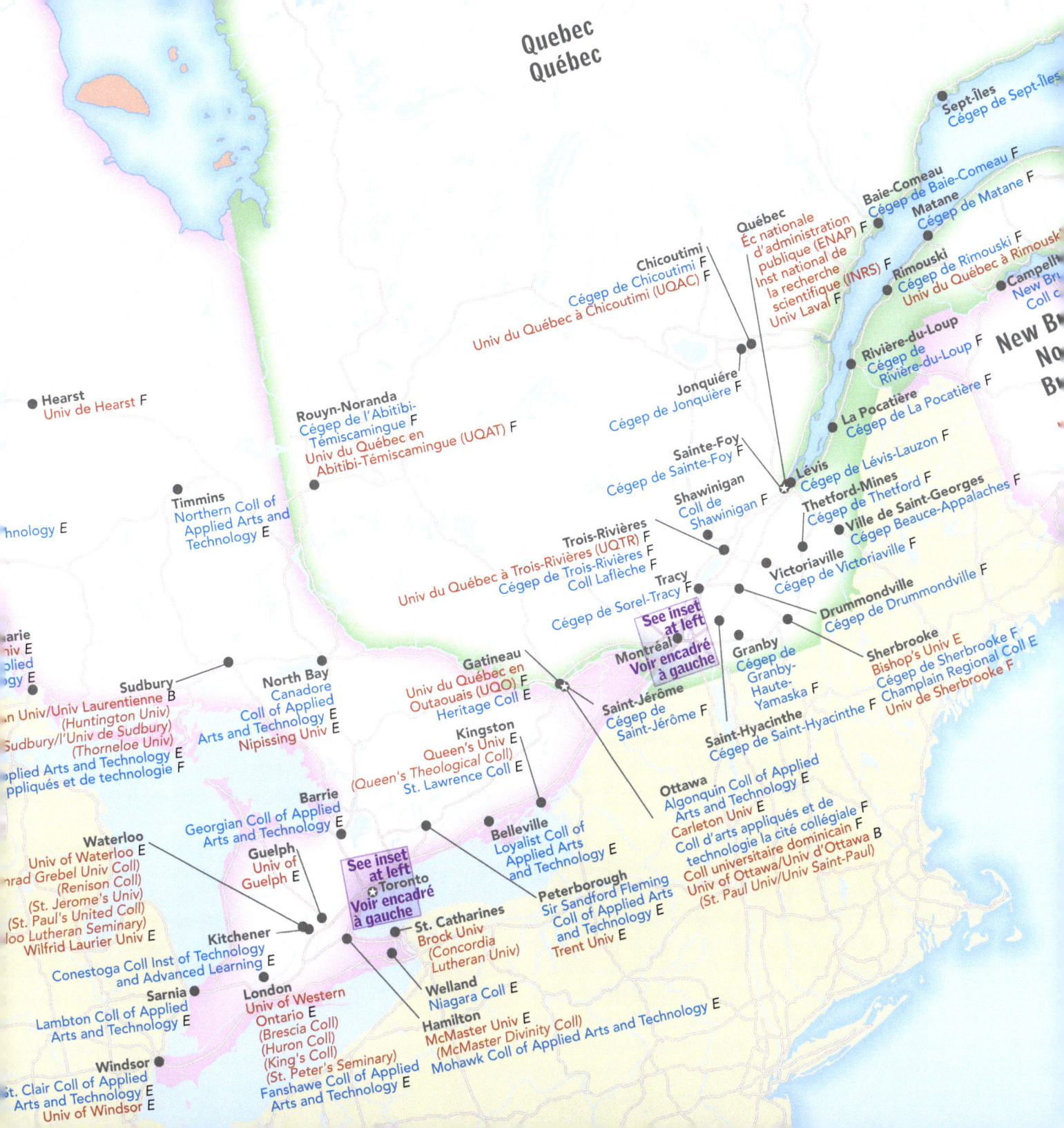

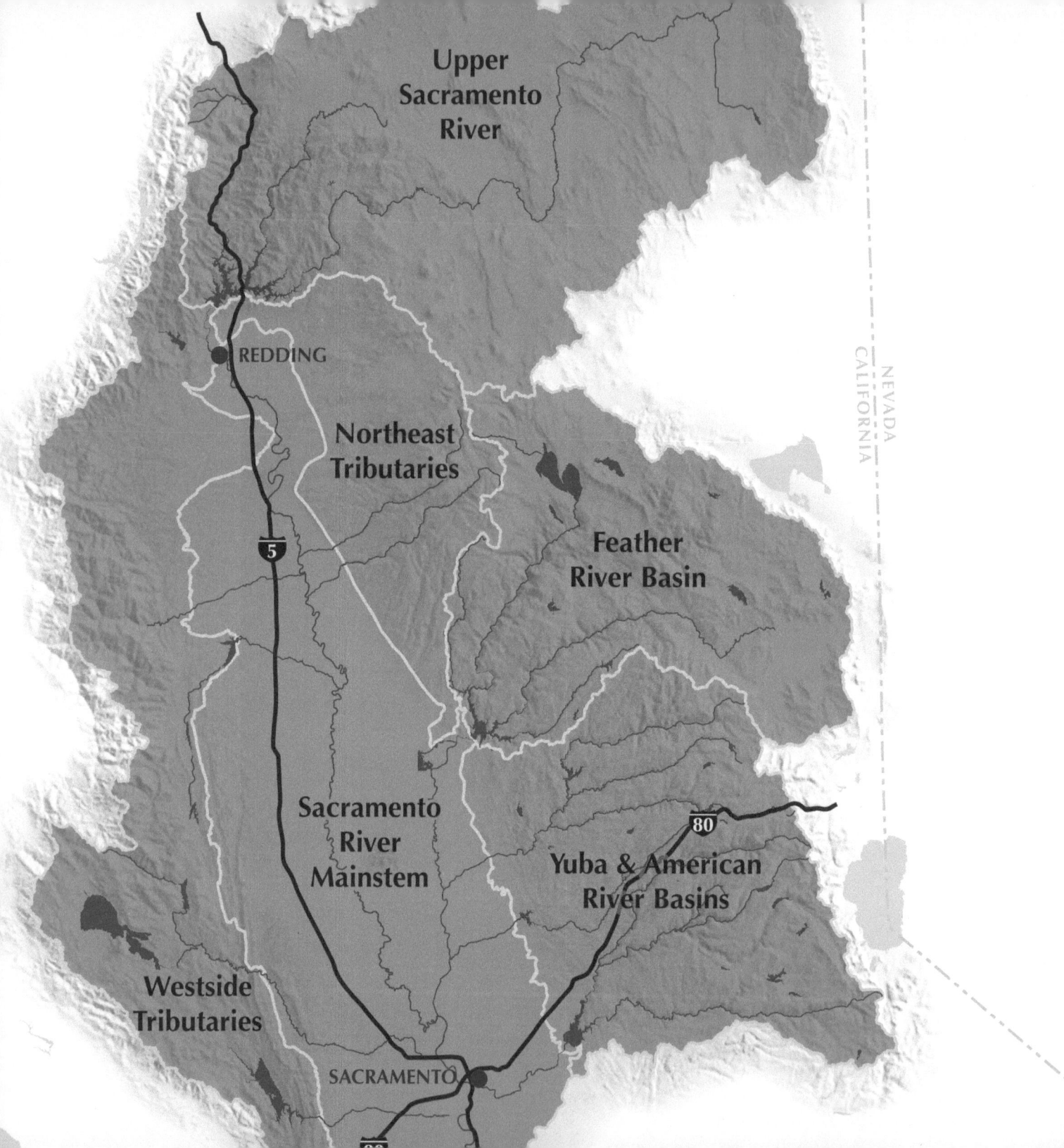

Upper
Sacramento
River

REDDING

Northeast
Tributaries

Feather
River Basin

I-5

Sacramento
River
Mainstem

Yuba & American
River Basins

80

Westside
Tributaries

SACRAMENTO

NEVADA
CALIFORNIA

David Medeiros, Medeiros Cartography

Sacramento River Watershed

Software Used: ArcGIS, MAPublisher, Adobe Illustrator, Natural Scene Designer

More information: www.mapbliss.com

Part of a contract job for the Sacramento River Watershed Program to produce publication maps from supplied GIS data for an upcoming "Atlas" of the watershed. Map submitted is one in a series of maps designed to illuminate the geography and issues of the Sacramento River Watershed. This map is the main watershed locator illustrating the main and sub watershed boundaries.

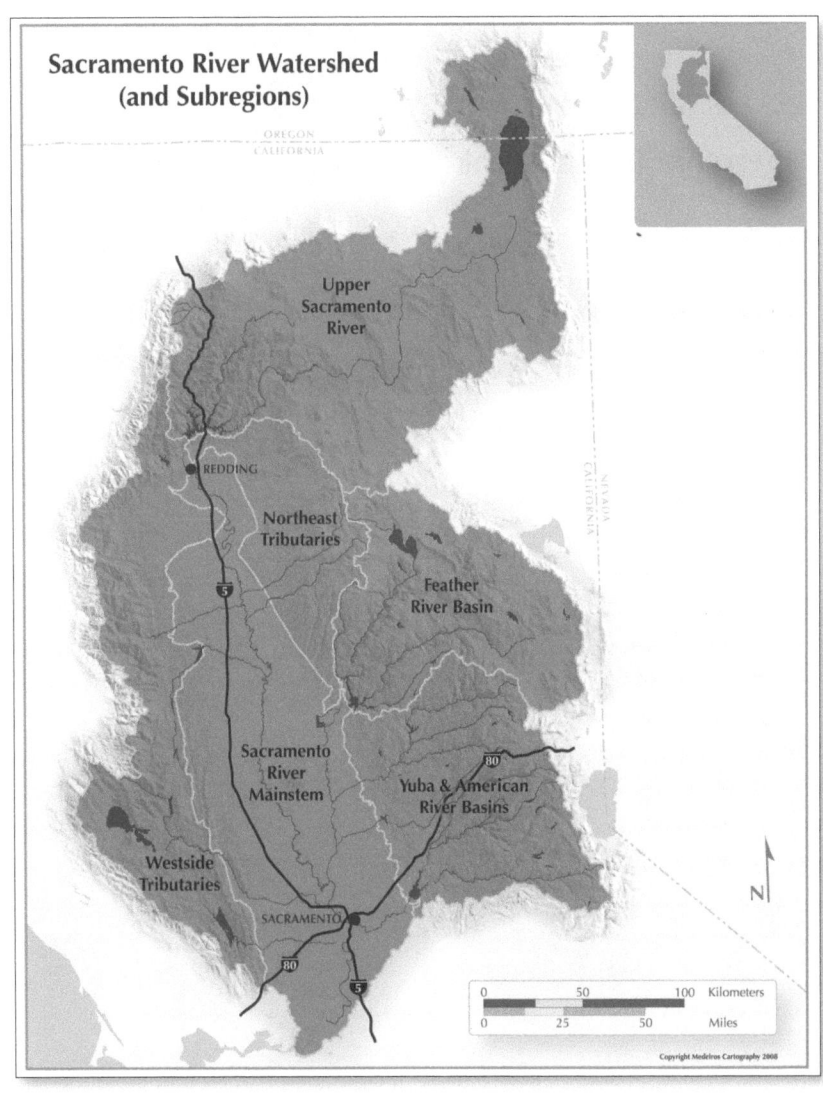

Gene Thorp, The Washington Post

Terror at Dismal Creek

Copyright © 2008 The Washington Post

Software used: Illustrator, Photoshop, Vectorworks with Azimuth Plug-in, ESRI ArcInfo, Google Earth, Natural Scene Designer

More information: www.washingtonpost.com, www.mapmanusa.com

This map was created to go along with a powerful story in the Washington Post newspaper about convicted murderer who was released after serving his sentence and tried to kill again. Instead of creating the perspective part of the graphic in Bryce3D, I experimented in using Google Earth in conjunction with other programs to get the desired effect.

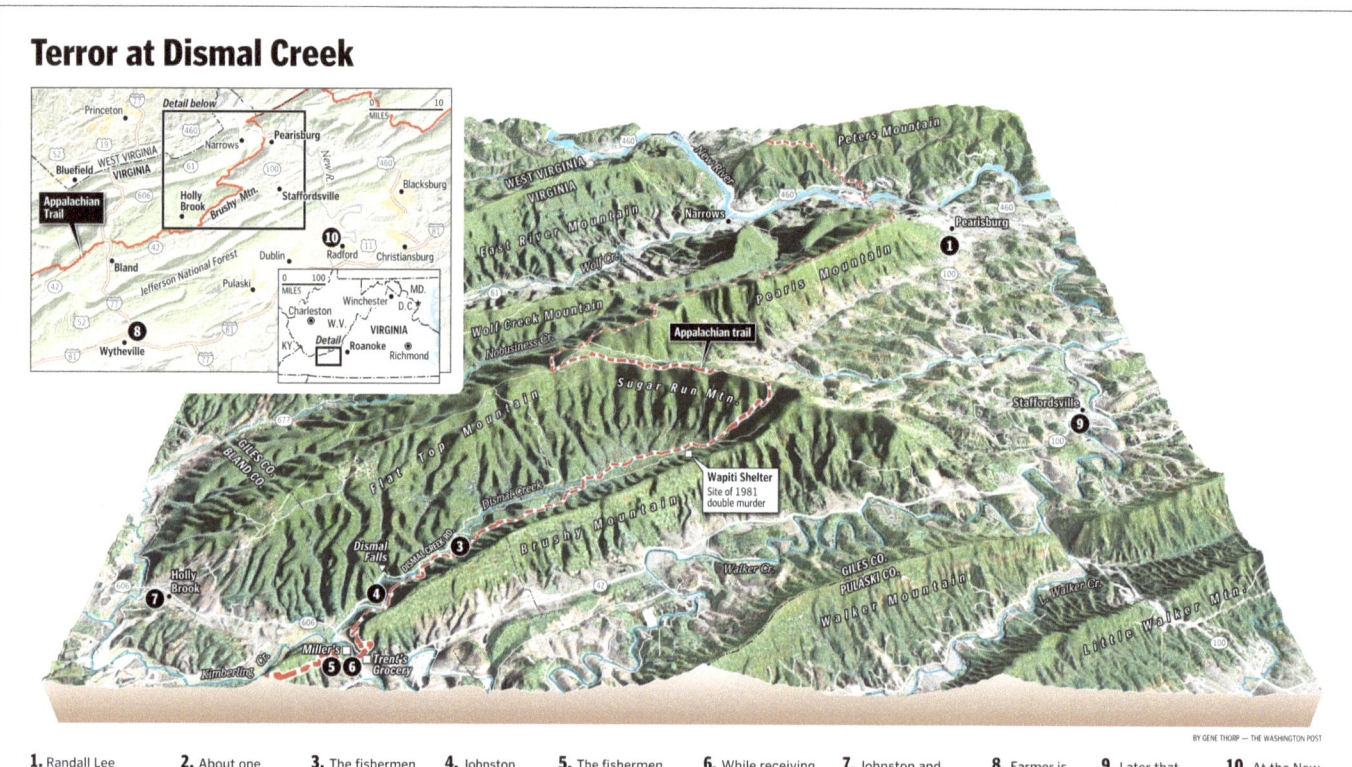

Terror at Dismal Creek

BY GENE THORP — THE WASHINGTON POST

1. Randall Lee Smith, a convicted murderer who was released from prison after serving his sentence, is reported missing from his house on April 30. Uncollected mail suggests Smith has not been home for almost two months.

2. About one week later, two fishermen, Scott Johnston and Sean Farmer, encounter Smith while on a camping trip at Dismal Creek. They are unaware of Smith's history.

3. The fishermen feed Smith and his dog at their campsite. Just after dark, Smith pulls a handgun from his pocket and shoots the two men several times, wounding both seriously.

4. Johnston and Farmer escape in Farmer's truck. They speed down the valley looking for help. Both struggle to stay conscious from a loss of blood.

5. The fishermen stop at the first house they see with lights on, the residence of Melissa Miller. They plead for help in her front yard and she calls 911. The closest ambulance is in Bland, a town 20 miles away.

6. While receiving medical treatment, Johnston identifies Smith as the shooter from a missing persons photo brought to him from Trent's Grocery. The police put out an all-points bulletin for Smith.

7. Johnston and Farmer are taken by ambulance to Holly Brook to be airlifted to a hospital. Johnston is evacuated to Carilion Roanoke Memorial Hospital, but Farmer, too heavy for the helicopter, is taken a longer route.

8. Farmer is driven an additional 25 miles to Wytheville where a larger helicopter transports him to the same Roanoke hospital.

9. Later that night, Smith is spotted by a state trooper near Staffordsville driving Johnston's truck. He is apprehended nearby after crashing the stolen vehicle.

10. At the New River Valley Regional Jail on May 10, Smith is found unresponsive. He is pronounced dead at Pulaski County Hospital later that day.

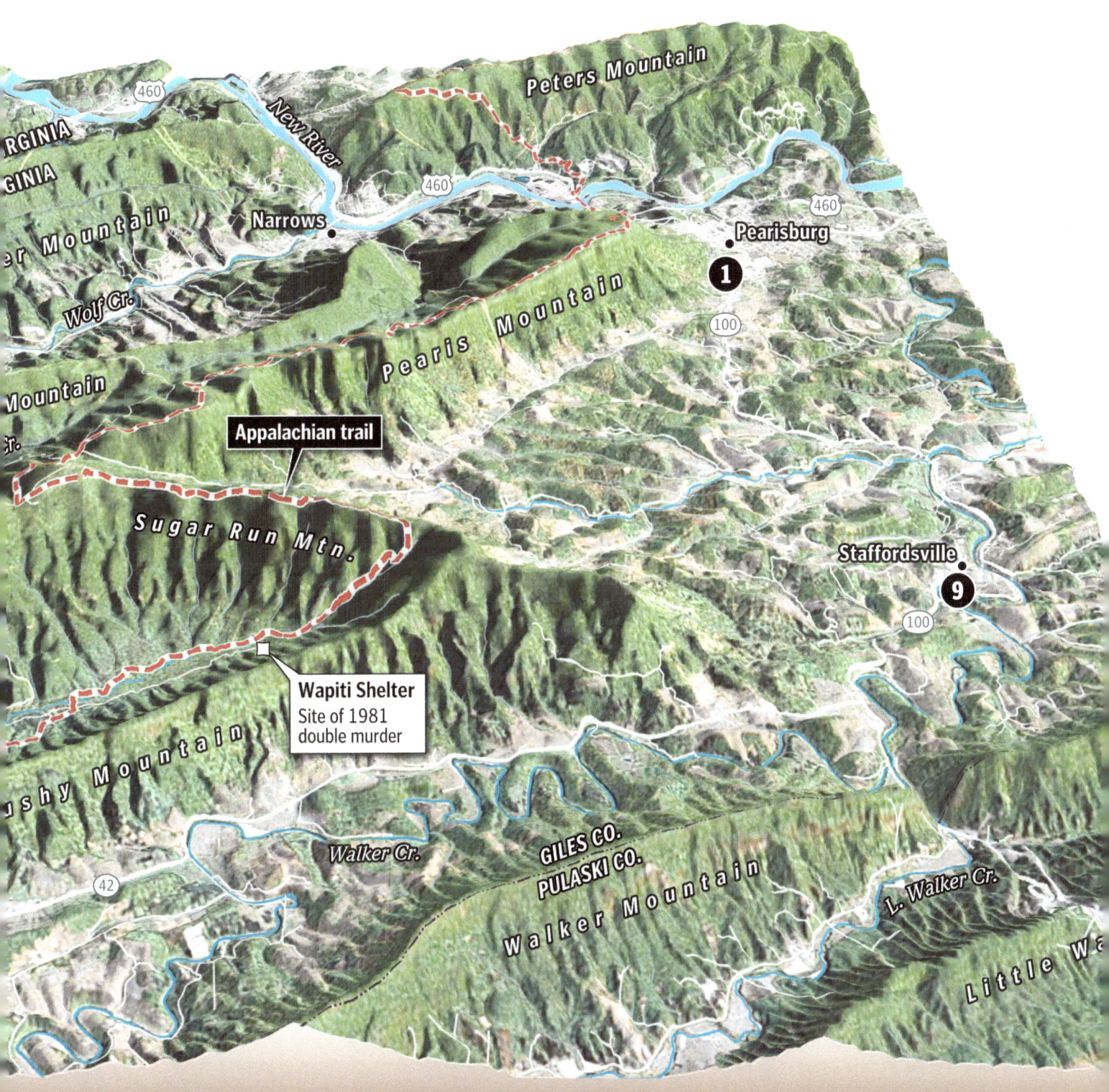

460

New River

460

460

VIRGINIA
GINIA

Peters Mountain

Narrows

Pearisburg

100

1

er Mountain

Wolf Cr.

Pearis Mountain

Mountain

cr.

Appalachian trail

Sugar Run Mtn.

Staffordsville

9

100

Wapiti Shelter
Site of 1981
double murder

ushy Mountain

Walker Cr.

GILES CO.
PULASKI CO.

L. Walker Cr.

42

Walker Mountain

Little Wa

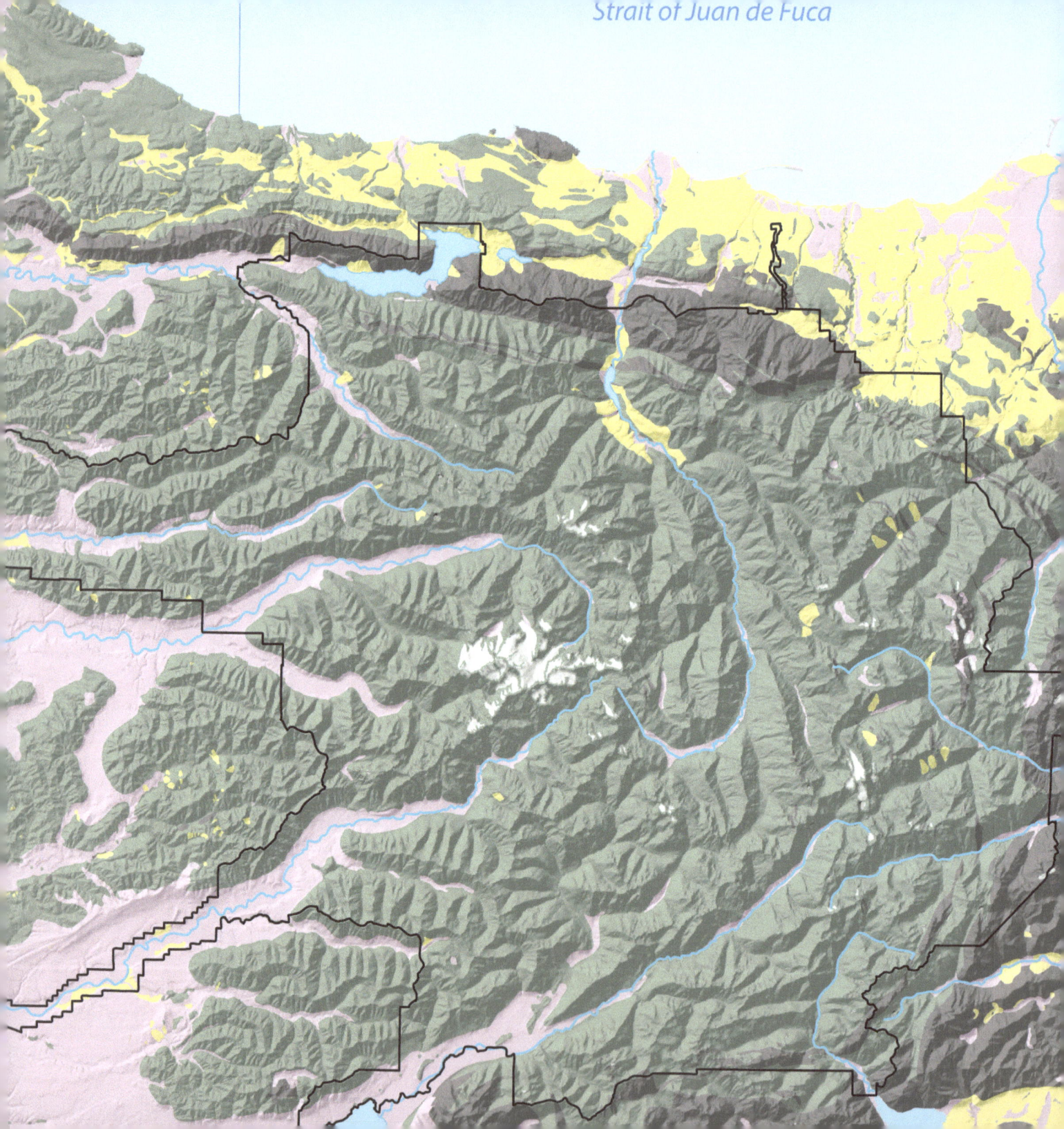

Strait of Juan de Fuca

Kristian R Underwood, KruCartographics

Generalized Geology ONP, Diptych I

Copyright: KruCartographics

Software Used: ArcMap 9.2, Adobe Photoshop and Illustrator CS3

This map was the first part of a diptych that was portrayed on the left facing page in the analysis of The Effects of Hillslopes on Trail Degradation, Olympic National Park, WA. It was used to illustrate my discussion of plate tectonics, glaciation, and the generalized geology of Olympic National Park and the surrounding peninsula. The geology layer was created from a detailed 1:100,000 geologic shapefile of the state of Washington. This layer was draped over a DEM/hillshade in Photoshop and the opacity was adjusted. Typology and layout was created in Illustrator

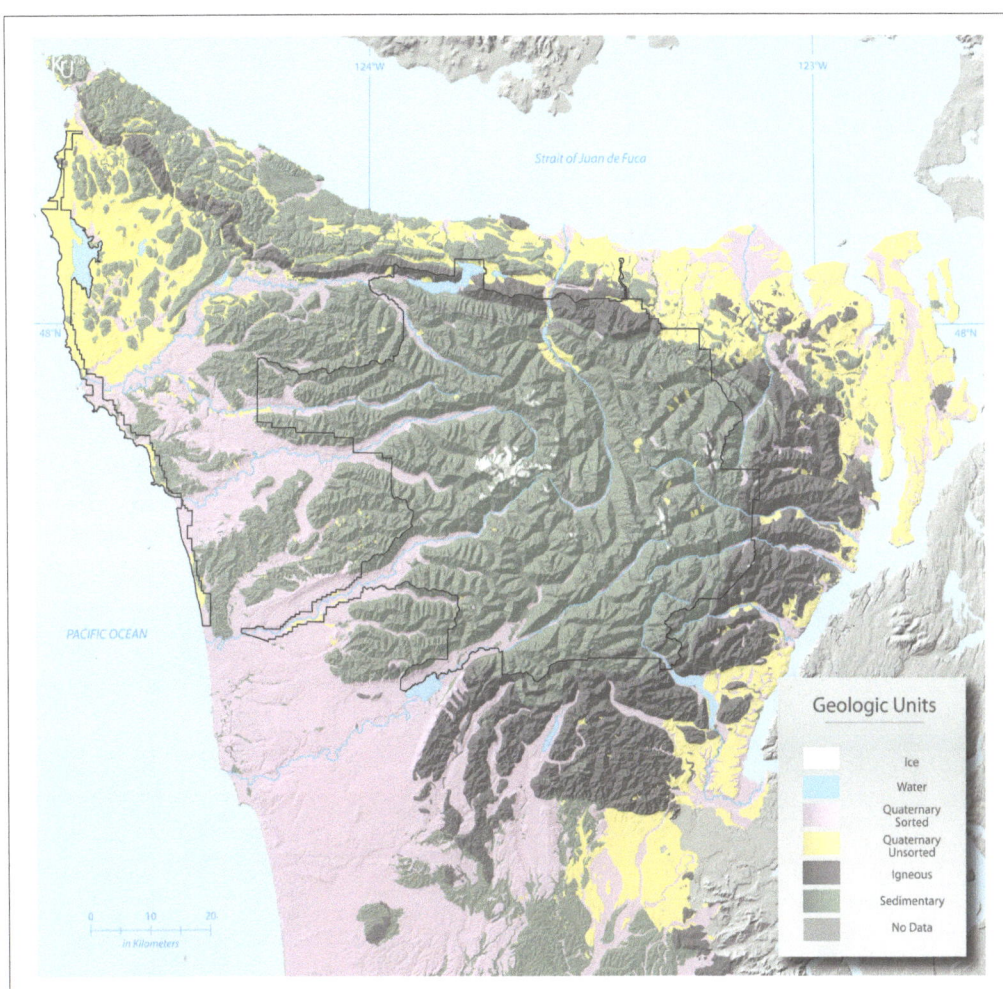

Figure 1-3: Major geologic terranes and glacial deposits of Olympic National Park (delineated in black) and Olympic Peninsula (data source, http://www.dnr.wa.gov/geology)

www.ingramcontent.com/pod-product-compliance
Lightning Source LLC
Chambersburg PA
CBHW051044180526
45172CB00002B/515